Life Between the Raindrops

Life
Between
the
Raindrops

L.E. HEWITT

SEABOARD PRESS

JAMES A. ROCK & COMPANY, PUBLISHERS

Life Between the Raindrops by L. E. Hewitt

SEABOARD PRESS

is an imprint of JAMES A. ROCK & CO., PUBLISHERS

Life Between the Raindrops copyright ©2008 by L.E. Hewitt

Special contents of this edition copyright ©2008 by Seaboard Press

Address comments and inquiries to:
SEABOARD PRESS
9710 Traville Gateway Drive, #305
Rockville, MD 20850

E-mail:
jrock@rockpublishing.com   lrock@rockpublishing.com
Internet URL: www.rockpublishing.com

Trade Paperback ISBN: 978-1-59663-659-0

Library of Congress Control Number: 2007941767

Printed in the United States of America

First Edition: 2008

Dedicated to
my father.

Thanks Dad
for my sense of humor
and for the wings you gave me.

I miss you every day.

CONTENTS

Preface

Life is a trek down an unexplored pathway. Each of us takes a different road. We become a product of what we experience along the way. I tend to look at life as a rainbow, full of many shades and colors. We all have dark moments and bright ones. Our best hope is that the good times outweigh the bad.

Life Between the Raindrops is a view of the world from where I live. If you find inspiration or smile a little, then this little book will have served its purpose. Hopefully, you will even be able to relate to some of the characters.

All of the characters in this book are real people. Only the names have been changed. Between the raindrops, my life is full of many interesting, unique subjects. I am certain yours is too.

So sit back, relax and enjoy. You are about to learn all about dancing in the outfield, the things mom forgot to tell you, the secrets of cold medicine, peanut butter & pickles and …

Elizabeth
the Baseball Star

Elizabeth came home from Kindergarten one day waving a paper in my face and proclaiming, "I want to do this! I want to do this!" It was a sign-up sheet for little league baseball. So we sat down and had the obligatory talk about commitment and how homework comes first and such. I do not think she really heard a word of it, but we had a deal and she was ready to leave her mark on the baseball world. Never having played baseball in her life, I had my work cut out for me in a short time period. We had to practice hitting and fielding and I had to teach her which bases to run in which order. My reputation as a father was on the line! I could not have the other dads looking down upon me because my kid ran the wrong direction. So I worked hard every evening to whip Elizabeth into shape. Over time she began to get a basic understanding of the game as well as a few bruises but finally we were ready!

She would be playing in a league where boys and girls played together and the coaches pitched. They wanted to promote success. Elizabeth was assigned to a team of about ten boys and three girls. But, by the third practice, the other two girls had quit. Elizabeth was unfazed. She was not bothered in the least about being the only girl on her team. In a way, I think it made her a favorite of the parents. In her first game, she struck out three times and stood attentively in right field. I considered that a success. It was something to build upon and most importantly she was having fun. As the season went on she did have some issues in the field. One day the coach had to ask her not do the Macarena while the other team was batting. Also, when a ball was hit in her direction, she would wait till it stopped rolling then pick it up and run to second baseman handing him the ball to throw. I think she thought he was cute.

Batting was a struggle. She had many strike outs. The few grounders she did hit were short and slow and she was tagged or thrown out every time. She was still having fun. Once or twice the games interfered with her social schedule and she had second thoughts, but in general, it was something she looked forward to. I felt she had gained a good understanding of the game. I was wrong.

It was just about the end of a long season. The game had gone on pretty typically. There were few runs and many errors. It was a good way to spend an early summer evening. The seven inning game was nearing an end. The opposing team was leading by one run. Time was running out. The first two batters were pop outs in the infield. These were desperate times. The pressure was on. The next batter got a hit up the middle, a nice single. This was followed by a grounder to third which was bobbled and kicked and then fallen upon, everybody safe!

So here we are. Two outs, two runners and Elizabeth was up next. A feeling against all hope came over the crowd. They all knew that she was zero for 127. She was in a hitting slump. Could she break out when it counted? The coach tossed the ball, and Elizabeth gave a mighty, closed eye swing, and WHACK! The ball went bounding between the first and second basemen! She had her first hit! And after a throwing error on the right fielder, the second baseman and the third baseman, the winning runs came home. Elizabeth was a hero! Congratulations all around!

In the post game team meeting Elizabeth was given applause, and the game ball and what is most important, a coupon for a free pizza! Every parent and every player was giving her congrats! I was one proud papa! She had stood in the face of enormous pressure with the weight of the world upon her shoulders and had come through in the clutch!

The moment I will never forget was yet to come. As we got in the car, Elizabeth asked me, "Dad, why was everybody congratulating me?" I then realized that she had felt no pressure at all. She had simply been playing for the sheer fun of it. It was then that I was most proud of all.

Hats

Today I am riding a bus traveling from Pennsylvania to Tennessee. One of my favorite ways to pass the time during a journey like this is to observe the various traveling companions with whom I am sharing this ride in a torture chamber. I am seated near the rear today. So all I can really see is the top half of the backs of people's heads.

The thing that catches my eye is the hats I see. At least half of the men I can see are wearing one sort or another, yet I do not see one single woman with one.

Interesting. Hats used to be a big thing with women, kind of a fashion statement, especially when dressing in more formal attire. Nowadays, however, it is a rarity with the notable exception of little old ladies on Sundays. I wonder why women have abandoned the use of hats.

Now those Sunday ladies offer a whole different curiosity for me. I want to know where in the heck they ever found some of those hats and what ever possessed them to buy them! Was this an impulse purchase after nipping too much cider which had turned hard at the women's auxiliary meeting? Did they lose a bet? Or maybe they had a collision with a bird while driving a convertible to church. And yet they come strutting in looking all proud and stuff. Almost seems like there should be an emcee down front. "Here comes Widow Thompson in her lovely lavender sequined, midi-length dress with off-the-shoulder sleeves and white-knitted shawl. The ensemble is accented by the ass end of three peacocks on her head. Doesn't she look smashing this morning folks?"

Anyhow, back to the guys on the bus. I suppose there are many different reasons for hats, from utilitarian to fashion to making an advertising statement. I also would bet that baldness is the driving force in a lot of hat sales as well. I have a few baseball style caps myself. They all advertise something, a sports team or a local business etc. ... These have sort of become the standard and that is true of the people on this bus as well. It is winter time and while not really cold, there are a couple of toboggan wearers among us as well. The ones that interest me most are the more unique hats in the crowd.

One fellow with silver hair is wearing what I believe you would call a fedora—a stylish sort of dressy, old-fashioned hat. Another guy, probably thirty-something, has on a sort of flat brimmed, leather bandito hat. I do not know the official name for it, but it is kind of like a bad-assed cowboy hat. The kind the bad guys usually wore in those old western movies. These two guys each bought their hats with a certain look or statement in mind and that is cool. Maybe I need to put some thought into a special style of hat that expresses who I am. I wonder how an Abe Lincoln top hat would go over at the golf course. Or maybe I will just let the old ladies at the church pick out something special for me.

Annie

Annie came into this world at the tail end of the baby boom, born to loving parents best described as working poor. In a little house full of love, if not a lot of money, she was the baby of the family, loved and pampered by all. Her childhood was spent in a small village of a couple hundred people, a few miles down the road from town and many miles from the nearest city. She was raised to be quite proper in hopes that her future might be more glamorous than the simple existence of her parents. They were good people, honest and friendly in all their endeavors. They taught Annie respect and manners and the meaning of common decency. She did well in school. She was never a problem. She was growing up to be a good kid. Well respected in the community. A child of promise.

She was not very old, about 10 or so I guess, when it became apparent that she had a natural ability to sing. With no formal training, she had true pitch and rich tone to her young voice. So with the support of her family, she began to sing publicly at church and school and then various social functions. She was building a dream and honing her craft. And she was beginning to gain fans along the way. Again, this was a child of promise.

My first encounter with her was when she was 16—her 16th birthday party, as a matter of fact. I was the drummer in a band that had been asked to play for her party. There was no money involved—just a favor for a friend and the promise of free food. Many times when we would play at informal events, people from the audience would get up to sing. They were amateurs for the most part, but it was all in good fun. So when they said Annie was gonna sing a couple songs, I thought little of it—just another school girl who sang in the choir. But from the moment she opened her mouth to sing, I knew this was no ordinary girl.

As it turned out, I was going to be turning 16, myself, in three months. I too had led a wonderful childhood in a poor family. I too was the baby. I had already been playing music in public for six ½ years at this point and felt like an "old pro." I had big aspirations for my music and was constantly playing with musicians who were much older. This often made me the center of attention and I liked it that way. I was not accustomed to anybody else stealing my spotlight.

The song I remember most from that day was" Crazy." It was originally written by Willie Nelson and sung by Patsy Cline and while I had heard many singers try over the years to sing it, they always fell short of the original. It required such vocal control that many singers did not even attempt it. Now, standing in before me, was this 16-year-old who not only *attempted*, but nailed it! Even if she was standing in my spotlight, this girl had promise!

We were introduced that day and chatted a bit but that was the last we would encounter one another until I was 19. As a seasoned veteran of 10 years in the music business, it was now time for me to form my own band with my own plans. I had worked for many others, but now knew the direction in which I wanted to go with my musical career. I was ready to assemble the brightest and best I could find and put together the act to lead me to the top of my profession. And I knew just where to start. I made the phone call and arranged to meet with Annie and her parents to discuss my plans.

We spent most of that summer together gathering new members through auditions, practicing our songs, and socializing. I had found a new friend. We enjoyed one another's company and did many things together. We would laugh and talk for hours, but our favorite activity was going to Denny's to stuff our faces with breakfast food late at night. We were two of a kind.

Annie was very feminine in her ways, never a hair out of place, always in makeup, always proper. Yet she had a great ability to hang out with the guys, to just kind of fit in. This was a great asset to the band. Her breathy, rich voice made her an instant success and was a great drawing card for the band's engagements. I felt this was the life she was destined to live and that her future was written in the stars. The band was a huge success. Our popularity grew with each performance. Annie and I had both realized a dream and were living it on stage. Unfortunately, nightclub bands are often short lived ventures. Mixing five or six personalities into a sort of family is often difficult. So after a couple of years the band broke up. I, of course, simply moved on to the next act and the next venture and kept moving. But Annie did not. She seemed to take it hard. And even though several others and I tried to involve her in new projects, she never took that step again. I could not understand why she was wasting her wonderful talent.

During this time her father had passed away. This left Annie and her mother at home. I think she felt a need to stay there and care for her aging mother before venturing out to pursue her own life. She did not wish to see her mother alone. So she settled into a regular office job leading a normal sort of life.

I went on about my life and slowly lost contact with Annie. Always thinking, "I need to call her sometime." But the call I never made came my way one Saturday morning. Not from Annie, but from her mother, informing me that Annie had been in a very bad car wreck and had passed away. At age 40 she was gone. I never got to make that call as I had intended to for so many years. She still lived at home with her mother. She was still there doing what she thought was right. As it turns out, her mother soon followed passing within a few months. I am certain the pain was simply too much to bear.

When I think back now, I realize that I was right when I said her future was written in the stars. Annie's talents were much too great for this humble existence.

My Day

I decide to water my garden.

As I turn on the hose in the driveway, I look over at my car and decide my car needs washing.

As I start toward the garage, I notice that there is mail on the porch table that I brought up from the mail box earlier.

I decide to go through the mail before I wash the car.

I lay my car keys down on the table, put the junk mail in the garbage can under the table, and notice that the can is full.

So, I decide to put the bills back on the table and take out the garbage first.

But then I think, since I'm going to be near the mailbox when I take out the garbage anyway, I may as well pay the bills first.

I take my checkbook off the table, and see that there is only one check left.

My extra checks are in my desk in the study, so I go inside the house to my desk where I find the can of soda that I had been drinking.

I'm going to look for my checks, but first I need to push the Coke aside so that I don't accidentally knock it over.

I realize the Coke is getting warm, and I decide I should put it in the refrigerator to keep it cold.

As I head toward the kitchen with the Coke, a vase of flowers on the counter catches my eye. They need to be watered.

I set the Coke down on the counter, and I discover my reading glasses that I've been searching for all morning.

I decide I better put them back on my desk, but first I'm going to water the flowers.

I set the glasses back down on the counter, fill a container with water and suddenly I spot the TV remote. Someone left it on the kitchen table.

I realize that tonight when we go to watch TV, I will be looking for the remote, but I won't remember that it's on the kitchen table, so I decide to put it back in the den where it belongs, but first I'll water the flowers.

I pour some water in the flowers, but quite a bit of it spills on the floor.

So, I set the remote back down on the table, get some towels and wipe up the spill.

Then I head down the hall trying to remember what I was planning to do.

At the end of the day the driveway is flooded, the car isn't washed, the bills aren't paid, there is a warm can of Coke sitting on the counter, there is still only one check in my checkbook, I can't find the remote, I can't find my glasses, and I don't remember what I did with the car keys.

Then when I try to figure out why nothing got done today, I'm really baffled because I know I was busy all day long, and I'm really tired.

A Wiser Way
to Spend Money

I watched a story today on one of the news channels about the humanitarian crisis in Somalia. They are having civil unrest which is contributing to lack of food and shelter. Relief workers were passing out plastic tarps for the people to cover their stick huts to provide some protection in the upcoming rainy season. They were not passing out any food. This was what was needed most. The poor children looked malnourished. Old ladies were begging for food saying they had not eaten in days.

I also read a story today about the cost of military operations being conducted in Iraq and Afghanistan. It was estimated currently at more than 150 billion dollars. I cannot even imagine that kind of money. I understand the basic need for a military and defense. I also know people are quite divided on how the war on terror is being waged. But, can we agree on one thing? Could the military spare two billion dollars? That is less than 1.5 % of the current expenditure in the war. Just a small cutback here or there.

These figures are off the top of my head, but let's be generous. Let's say it takes $200 million to safely deliver food to these people.

It could be much, much less, but I am being generous. That would leave $1.8 billion to buy food. They said there were about two million hungry people there. That is $900 dollars for each of them. I have a family of five. If I went to the grocer and spent $4500, we could eat for a long time! I am willing to bet if you were spending 1.8 billion you could get a big discount. Kroger, Wal-Mart, Publix, and all the others could fight it out for your business.

Another benefit would be the feeling of goodwill generated around the globe. I bet a policy of helping the least fortunate would in time reduce the need for so much military spending. People would begin to like the United States and what it stands for. The "little guy" around the world would begin to stand up to defend our honor because we helped him in his greatest time of need. This policy would save countless lives.

Some will say we need to remain strong to protect our way of life. They will debate that taking from the military will put us at risk. That is OK too. We can find other ways of funding this venture. We can individually look at our selfish ways and make minor changes to change the world. How much is your cable television bill? I read that the FCC estimates the average household spends $40/month. I also did a little digging and found that in 2002, there were more than 60 million subscribers. Let's see 60,000,000 x $40 = $2.4 billion every month! Can you make do on three channels and rabbit ears? Or would you rather those kids starve to death and live in a stick hut. The only difference between them and you is where you were born. You got lucky they did not.

I am not picking on the cable industry either. I am simply using them to make a point. We live in the land of plenty and claim to be so religious and righteous while we knowingly let others suffer and die. It is not right. Things have got to change! Look in the mirror! Some would say, "Let the rich do it!" and while I agree that the rich can give more than the poor, we all can give a little. A small sacrifice is all it would take.

So tonight when you look at your kids, or your wife, or your parents, or whoever is important to you, just think. What if it were them in need? Or would you rather turn a blind eye while eating a steak in front of a big screen in air conditioning?

John's Golfing Adventures

John started playing golf during middle age. At least that is when he began to play frequently enough to even mention. He was a bachelor and this became his passion. He practically lived at the course during his free time. As with many amateurs, he would often make the same mistakes repeatedly. It would cause him great frustration and he would get angry and curse at himself and his clubs. During these times, he would often bang the club hard against the ground or fling it high into the air. But fate would break him of this habit one bright, hot summer afternoon.

He was playing in a foursome of friends and coworkers. The first few holes had gone relatively smoothly for him. He was playing bogey golf, which was about as good as he could expect consistently. Toward the end of the front nine, he began to develop a vicious slice on his tee shots. The ball would travel straight for about one hundred yards and then make a hard right turn, traveling at almost a right angle to the fairway. This was losing him distance and giving him poor lies in the rough or trees or bushes. His frustration and temper were beginning to show. After lunch at the turn, his hope was for a return to his better, if imperfect, form. But things were going downhill fast.

Golf is such a mental exercise that when something like this happens to your swing, it becomes a self-serving prophecy. You get into this zone where you cannot get the problem out of your mind often exacerbating the problem. As things went from bad to worse, John began hitting more and more shots poorly. Now it was not just his driver, but his fairway irons as well. He would hit a big slice, reach in his pocket, drop another ball and hit another big slice. He would sometimes hit three or four balls from the same spot getting madder by the minute.

By the time he reached the fourteenth, he was at wit's end. This was a dogleg right with some woods along the right and pines along the left. If he could just straighten it out a little, he could make the bend in the fairway work for him. He teed it up, gave it a rip and watched it sail deep into the woods on his right. The slice was so bad you thought the ball was coming backwards toward the end of its flight.

Without a word, he teed up another and gave it a wicked rap. It landed about ten feet from the first. He slammed the head of the club into the ground repeatedly while the other three players chuckled in the background. A third time he teed it up. Same results. You could have thrown a large blanket over all three of them. A fourth time. This time there was a change. It sliced even deeper than the first three!

He then turned shouting some expletives at himself and flung his driver high into the air. It flew a good thirty-five or forty feet upward before beginning its fall, landing right in the top of one of those pines on left, twenty feet off the ground. He stood there perplexed while the others broke into full belly laughter. Then, without a word, realizing the error of his ways, not to mention the price of the driver, he began to climb that tree all the way to the top to get his club back.

That was ten years ago. John still gets mad at himself on the course. He still slams his club down and curses at himself. But his throwing days seem to be over.

The Amish
at the Flea Market

I enjoy browsing through yard sales and flea markets. You find such an amazing variety of stuff. It is an educational archive of our culture. I love just digging around looking for the bits of treasure there just waiting to be discovered. Meg's house is three quarters of a mile up the road from a nice country flea market. We sometimes go to visit her on weekends and will stop by there to see what things we can find. Meg also lives in an area where there are a significant number of Amish and Mennonite communities. So it is very common to see a horse and buggy on her road. This past Saturday morning was no exception.

Meg's two small dogs were out in the yard taking care of business when they began barking. I looked out the window to see what was the commotion. There was an Amish man on a horse drawn wagon full of mums headed for the flea market. Upon informing Meg, she was determined to go and pick up some for her own yard.

After breakfast we were off to the market. It is held in and around an open air building full of built in tables upon which the vendors spread their goods. It is a bustling place full of activity. As we entered the parking lot, the wagon I had seen going by the house was parked near the front entrance. It was teeming with beautiful, large baskets of mums in a variety of colors. Meg said we would stop there last.

As we made our way amongst the vendors, I spotted trouble straight ahead. Someone had beagle puppies. Meg falls in love with every animal she sees. Even though she has two dogs, two cats, and a hamster, I knew this was gonna be touch and go. And sure enough, as soon as she spotted them, she was like a moth to the flame. She petted and hugged and kissed and loved on each and every one of the litter of six. She was twenty minutes trying to convince herself that she could not do without one. Finally she decided to walk around the rest of the market while she contemplated what to do.

The pups were in a makeshift pen of chicken wire set up in the gravel lot with a bowl of water and a pet carrier. It was a nice fall day and they were reasonably comfortable. Not enough for Meg though. We had become separated while snooping through the market, but when I found her again, she was back at the pups having bought them some old sweatshirts to lie upon. She was concerned about their comfort. So even though she did not purchase one to take home, she did spend another fifteen minutes making sure they were all comfy upon their makeshift bed.

Finally, it was off to the flower wagon. We explained to the gentleman how we had seen him earlier and he and Meg took part in a neighborly chat while she made her selections. Jokingly, as she paid him, she told him he could leave any unsold flowers at her house on his way home.

The plan for that day included cleaning and sealing her wooden deck on the back of her house. So we made our way back home with our purchases kind of dreading the hard work ahead of us. Yes, it was a hard day. The large deck appeared about thirteen miles long as we scrubbed and sprayed and scrubbed some more.

Into the afternoon we worked, the recreational morning long forgotten. As we neared the end of our ordeal, we came up about a quart short of one of the chemicals we were using, requiring a quick trip to the hardware store. Meg told me to go ahead while she hosed off the last of what we had done.

As I rounded the end of the house toward the driveway, I stopped dead in my tracks. I then turned and went to retrieve Meg. I said to her that I was gonna bring a big smile to her face. I took her by the hand and led her round to the drive where she could see two large baskets of mums, one on each side of the end of her drive, which had been left by the Amish man on his wagon ride home.

Computer Talk

I have been suffering with a pain in my lower back and lower abdomen for the past several days. It has been a kind of soreness and aching feeling. This is a holiday weekend and I intended to tough it out until Monday so I could go see my regular doctor, but last night the pain worsened and I became concerned that it might be something serious, so this morning I went to the local emergency room to be seen. After much testing, I was diagnosed with Piriformis Syndrome. It is a sort of muscle spasm running from the center of the back to the inside of the hip. The ER doctor's recommendation was for me to take a prescription muscle relaxer and to make an appointment with a chiropractor.

Upon returning home, I logged onto the internet site of my health insurance company to obtain the names of some contracted chiropractors in my area. I spent a good thirty minutes fruitlessly trying to convince the computer to surrender the desired information. I found family practitioners, urologists, ob/gyns, internists, and a whole host of other specialties. Finally, I gave in. I was gonna have to just call the 800 number.

I dialed the number and a sweet, helpful, accommodating,

young lady answered the phone on the second ring. Come on! Get real! When does a human being ever answer a customer service number at a large company? Instead I was forced to battle wits with another computer. By this time I had given up on finding the correct information in its data files. My goal was to break through its security and actually talk to a person.

The computer was operating on a voice prompt system. It asked my name, my address, my ID number, my checking account number, my mother's shoe size. It asked if I was calling about medical, dental, or mental health services. It was full of questions when I would have been much better served if it had simply shut up and listened to my one question and then given me the answer I desired! Finally I decided I was gonna have to try and play along to satisfy this machine's ego.

"Please choose from the following options," the computer queried. "Are you calling for information about medical, dental or mental health services?"

I said, "I am calling to speak to a human."

" Sorry, I did not get that," it replied. "Please choose from the following options. Are you calling for information about medical, dental or mental health services?"

I debated this question for a moment. Should I bypass all the contributory steps and go straight to mental health services? Won't we all end up on the therapist's couch as victims of mental abuse inflicted by these damned computers anyhow? Why fight it? Go ahead and get an appointment for some pills that make the world a happy place. I was quite tempted, but I decided to stand my ground and fight.

"Medical!" I stated.

"Do you desire information on coverage, benefits, participating physicians, or which year to expect a denial notification letter for your most recent claim due to a typographical error by our data input clerk?" the computer responded with what I construed as a smug attitude.

I tried the benefits option. Then, all the computer did was tell me I did, indeed, have coverage that had been in effect since 2002. Based upon the given choices, I then chose "Main Menu" taking me back to the previous choices. I was losing my patience. This time I chose "Benefits." I was then prompted to make a choice as to what sort of benefit problem the computer could help me with. I listened intently to the 43 choices, none of which was what I was looking for. I sat there exasperated trying to plot my next move. At that moment, however, Buckshot entered the room and saved the day.

Buckshot is the resident schnauzer, beggar, and barker around the house. Just as the computer asked me which option I wanted, Buckshot barked.

The computer heard him and responded, "For this condition, it will be necessary to speak with a customer service specialist to further assist you. Please hold while I transfer you to the next available representative."

I was amazed! The dog was able to accomplish what I could not! So my advice is the next time you need to call the insurance company, let the dog do the talking. Or if you do not have a dog, just bark intently into the phone.

The
School Dance

Elizabeth is attending her first school dance this afternoon. She began middle school last week. I guess it is sort of a right of passage. She has been excited about this all week. I asked why she wanted to go. She said because her friends were going.

I asked, "Are you going to dance?"

"No!" came her immediate reply, as if I should have known better.

So I then asked, "What was she going to do there?" She explained she was going so she could talk to her friends. I then asked if these were the same friends she talked to all the time at school and on the phone. She just looked at me like I was stupid. Of course they were!

"What are you going to talk about?" I inquired.

"Nothing!" she said, becoming a bit agitated with my barrage of questions.

"And this is gonna cost me five bucks?" I asked.

At this point Shelly, her older sister chimed in. "Dad don't you know anything!" she said. Being in eighth grade, she is a veteran of these affairs.

"Nobody goes there to dance. You go there to hang out with your friends. The boys pretty much stay on one side of the room, and the girls on the other. They just kinda stare at each other across the floor." She continued. "You just listen to the music and talk! So cough up the money!"

"Tell you what! I will turn on the stereo and you can invite your friends over here to the house. And I will only charge them $2.50 each!" I explained.

"Dad! No!" they responded in unison.

"I am saving them money!" I pleaded.

"No!" came the forceful response.

I love being a dad. It is so much fun! And of course I coughed up the cash.

Meg's Kindness

Meg is a wonderful woman. She embodies so many of the qualities I admire. Her kind, caring, sharing nature is a beautiful thing. She is physically attractive—blond hair, blue eyes, trim, fit—and a treat for the senses. She is also very businesslike. She has a tough steely nature about her personality. She is a doer or a fixer so to speak. She sees something that needs done and she just does it. She has the need to rely on no one. And she can be tough as nails when she needs to be.

Life has made her tough. Her kindness has often been taken advantage of. It has caused her to hide that beautiful kind soul more and more over the years. However, it does still show at times and those are truly special moments.

I have known Meg for probably five or six years. She was a business acquaintance who became a friend and in the past year became my best friend. She is not perfect. None of us are. She makes mistakes and missteps. But the selfless acts that she performs are a great example of how we all should live.

I was present for one of these moments late one night in a Denny's restaurant. She and I were sitting at a corner table chatting and waiting for our food. For some reason she seemed a bit distracted. I did not give it much thought. I just assumed she was tired. But then all of a sudden, she got up from our table and went to another immediately behind us and put a $20 bill on the table occupied by four teenaged boys.

All she said to them was, "You've gotta save at least two dollars for the tip."

Turns out she had overheard them talking about being very short on cash and trying to order the cheapest things they could find on the menu. She did not know them at all and they were not asking anybody for help, but she was able to make that selfless gesture and do something I bet they will never forget. I thought that was very special.

On another occasion, we were at a Waffle House. It was shift change time and the server who was going off duty had been sitting there waiting for her ride home. Meg noticed her trying to call for someone to come get her. The girl seemed tired and distressed about how she was going to get home. Meg told me that if she was still there when we were through eating, then we were gonna give her a ride home. Fortunately, the girl's ride arrived just as we were about to get up from the table, but the selfless intentions that Meg had left a lasting impression on me.

One summer a mouse decided to set up residence in Meg's home. It also decided to have a family while it was there. Meg's steely exterior was the first thing you saw.

"I am gonna set some traps and get rid of those mice." she said.

They were leaving little presents all over her immaculately clean house and she was at her wit's end. My animal loving daughter pleaded with Meg to use glue traps so the mice could be caught then set free. Reluctantly Meg agreed. We helped her set out the traps and showed her how to use cooking oil to release her captives. Things were great until Meg caught a baby mouse.

"It is just a baby! It is so cute! I can't just put it outside for something to kill!" she said. Was this the same woman who had declared war on the mice a few days earlier? The baby mouse spent the next several days being fed, watered, petted and pampered until Meg deemed it old enough to survive in the wild—probably to spend his life telling his buddies where they could get a free meal and comfortable accommodations. So much for "tough as nails."

I have even witnessed Meg giving CPR to a frog who had tragically fallen into her pool. The poor thing appeared lifeless, but after 30 minutes of constant attention, it came back to life. And after another few hours of life in a plastic bucket, it was released hopping happily off into the bushes. How many people do you know who would go to such measures to save one of God's creatures?

Just the other day we were driving down a rural highway when we passed an old man selling pumpkins by the side of the road.

"Turn around!" Meg chimed.

"What is it?" I asked startled that something was wrong.

"I feel sorry for that old man" she said. "I want to buy some pumpkins from him." So back we went making a U-turn to pick out a couple of would be jack-o-lanterns. The old man seemed quite pleased as we pulled away having paid him more than the asking price. Not so steely after all is she?

If more of the world were like the real Meg, this would be one beautiful place to live.

Silence is Not Always Silent

I have been spending a lot of time at the hospital as of late with my ailing father. It is a constantly busy atmosphere of hustle and bustle. All types of unexpected visitors popping in from time to time for either social or professional reasons.

I have noticed though, that about one hour prior to the afternoon shift change, the activity all just seems to stop. I am sure that the doctors, nurses, therapists and such are all off somewhere catching up on paperwork, but for the patients, the place becomes like a ghost town. A good time for a nap.

For me, however, this has become an opportunity to examine the underlying sounds of a living, breathing hospital—chance to observe those noises which are always there, but go mostly unnoticed. It is amazing the amount of noise which is present within what is first perceived as silence.

The first sound I notice is the most constant one—the low rumble of the heat and air system. It is actually a sort of soothing, low frequency white noise. This is a sound familiar in most homes nowadays and can be quite comforting.

Another noise I am very aware of is coming from the clock on the wall above my head. A quite standard wall clock for a place like this, it is probably about fifteen inches in diameter with a white face and black hour, minute and second hands. A plain old hard-working clock. The reason it catches my attention is that it makes a kind of rattling click every two seconds as the second hand moves. I wonder why not every second or every three seconds? Is there a reason why it is every two?

My father's room is located next to a service elevator shaft. The intermittent hum of patients and supplies being transported from floor to floor is almost constant. They sure get a lot of use out of that one elevator. A short distance down the hall is the small office of a nursing administrator. His occasional phone conversations, while indecipherable, add to the environment as do the footsteps of the hallway pedestrians. The mixture is also enhanced by the frequent drone of the intercom system paging doctor so and so to call the operator.

All in all this peace and quiet is really very little of either one.

Ronson Hill Road

The Ronson Hill Road is an old, mainly unused gravel road winding down through some woods for a couple of miles and then connecting two country blacktop roads in rural Pennsylvania. The only automobile traffic to my knowledge is an occasional truck going back into the woods to check on a gas well.

For me, it is a road of many memories. It is the site of spring and fall hikes taken in my boyhood with my father. We would leave early in the morning and make an outing out of it packing a lunch and spending the splendid hours until early afternoon exploring the nature in this secluded paradise.

The day was filled with skipping rocks, swinging on grapevines, gathering leaves, watching squirrels, chipmunks, deer, rabbits, grouse, pheasants, and any number of other woodland creatures. Observing nature and the world as it exists outside of our "human" existence. The real world.

It was also the best opportunity I got to have the undivided attention of my dad. He was a good man and a great father, but like most adults he had too few hours in a day to accomplish all he needed to. He worked a forty-hour week and then came home to vegetable gardens and yard work and farm work on my grandfather's farm as well as home repairs and playing music at community events. He was a busy guy. He always took time to do things with my brother and me but those were typically shorter time periods plus I had to share him. This walk in the woods was the one large block of time where just he and I could have long discussions amid the fun things we did along the way.

These walks are a prime example of how the best memories of a childhood need not cost a dime. The most valuable gift he could offer me was his time. It was precious and I cherish those moments still all these years later.

I am sitting here right now thinking of this because it is late October and the air is crisp. It is a moment I will never again cherish with him, but I do hope to renew the tradition of that walk sometime in the next few years with someone special doing it in my father's memory

Diary
of a Virus

One of the side benefits of having school age children is that the beginning of each school year they bring home to you the latest virus to share. No matter how hard you try to avoid it, it's gonna get you. So here I sit, eyes all watery, nose running, scratchy throat, thanks to Shelly, my thirteen year old.

Of course she has also shared this with her siblings thereby creating more adventure for me. Elizabeth, who is eleven, has complained for three days now that her nose will not stop running. So I give her medicine, she complains it tastes bad. So I don't give her medicine. Then she complains that her nose won't stop running. Will, my nine year old, seemed to be escaping the plague until the car ride back from his favorite fast food joint. All he said was "Dad I feel sick" and before I could even get to a place to pull over, it was too late. At least his aim was good. He kept it confined to the floor mat. His case is keeping him from eating which could be considered a hidden blessing. I guess I could start him a college fund with the savings on this week's grocery bill.

As for me, I kept thinking about how the medicine I was taking would make me feel better for a while but how, after it wore off, I would actually feel worse than before I started. The thought crossed my mind that this was a good way to sell more medicine. What was in that stuff anyway? I got out the bottle and dug out the magnifying glass to read the ingredients. Low and behold, the first and therefore prominent ingredient was alcohol. The reason I was feeling bad was because I was suffering a hangover. At #3 on the list was sodium to run my blood pressure up. Number 5 was FD&C Blue no. 1 and #6 was FD&C Red no. 40. I am sure these colors are helping me feel better. Drink alcohol and lie around saying, "Oooooo see all the pretty colors." Next is high-fructose corn syrup to promote diabetes and at the end are three more sodium combinations to finish you off.

The one that most caught my attention was something called saccharin sodium. How is this drug contributing to my health? I wonder what other medicines this drug maker sells. It would seem quite advantageous for them to be in the blood pressure, diabetes, and cancer business.

Of course with all this in my system, I may not be thinking too clearly. But I have come to the conclusion that I am gonna cut out all these extras from my cure by making a trip to the liquor store. I will add in some sixties heavy metal music, buy a couple black light posters and a strobe light. See all those pretty colors? I ought to be feeling better in no time.

Dog Attack

Kent lived next door. He was about six or so and I was eleven. He had lived there for about two years. Even though he was younger, we played together a good bit. He was tough as nails and quite athletic so we found some common ground in various sports. We would play catch football and such. He was a very good kid.

I think part of the reason he spent a lot of time at my house is because things were not that good at his own. His parents fought a lot and seemed to struggle financially due to a lazy father. I think he just found my surroundings more pleasant and peaceful. He also seemed to have a knack for coming to visit just in time for supper. My mother would never turn him away and he often feasted on her wonderful concoctions.

I mentioned he was tough. I have never seen a kid so resilient. Kent would often fall and scrape a knee or elbow only to jump up and continue with whatever he was doing. But the episode I most remember sends chills down my spine. My yard had two rows of pines that lined the walkway from the garage to the house. The walkway was on a slope and there was a row above and below the path. We had laid cement slabs to create a sidewalk of sorts. One

of the pines on the upper side of the walkway had become dis-
eased and was removed. But as luck would have it, the school had
given out pines as a part of an Arbor Day celebration. I had proudly
planted the new seedling where the old tree had stood.

One of my favorite little stunts when on my way to the garage
was to run and hurdle the new tree, landing on the downslope
below it. The landing area was often about two-to-three feet lower
than the takeoff point so it was a tricky jump. Also as the years
went by it became more and more difficult as the tree grew taller.
Of course Kent wanted to do everything I did. And one day on
my way to the garage, I did my hurdle over the tree and kept
running. Kent, right behind me did the same.

While I did not see what happened, I certainly heard it. It was
a horrible SMACK! He had jumped the tree and fallen headfirst
into the concrete walkway. As I turned to see, I thought surely he
was dead or his head was broken in two! Kent jumped up, laughed,
and then took off running, beating me to the garage. I was amazed.

Kent's father did not care to work much, but he liked to go
hunting, especially raccoon hunting. People who raccoon hunt
typically do so in the middle of the night when these nocturnal
animals are out and about. They are hunted for their fur and they
are hunted with dogs. The dogs used for his purpose are very large
hounds. They follow the scent trail of a coon until they force it up
a tree. They then stand there and bark until the hunter comes
along to shoot the coon out of the tree. If the shot is not fatal, the
dogs will soon do him in.

As with any animal, if the dog is well cared for, it can be
friendly. Kent's father's laziness didn't make him a very good
caregiver. Therefore, some of his dogs were mean. One in particular would lunge at the end of his chain when anyone passed in its
sight. Many people had expressed their concern about its tem-

perament, but Kent's father always dismissed their concerns saying, "That dog would not hurt anybody." Even at eleven, I doubted that statement and felt he was in denial.

It came to pass that Kent and his family were going to be moving away. July 1st was to be the moving day. I did not know where they were moving or why, but I did know I would kinda miss Kent. We had some good fun together. On that morning, Kent came over wanting to play. The only thing was his mom had said he needed to play at his house rather than mine as we normally did. So I asked my parents if I could go over for a little bit since it was his last day here. They agreed and away we went. Out the back door, down through the yard and around the lower side of the garage. It was an old, free standing garage several yards from the house. And just on the other side was that dog lunging on the end of his chain as always. Kent and I were walking by when all of the sudden, the chain broke.

The dog headed straight for us. I knew his intentions were not good. I also knew I could not outrun him. So I turned to face him. He immediately lunged at my face. I reached out and grabbed whatever I could get a hold of. It was an ear. I was holding him down by his right ear! I knew this was all that was keeping me from a much less desirable outcome. He was still biting me relentlessly on the legs and buttocks, but I was buying time. Everything was moving in slow motion and was a blur.

I felt no pain, only a sort of warm, burning sensation. What seemed like an eternity was probably only about thirty seconds. Kent ran to his house to escape and get his mom who was eight months pregnant. She came running from one direction and my eighteen year old brother came running from the other. I thought to myself, "A few more seconds! Just hang on!" I could see help was on its way.

At that very point, the dog managed to snap its head around and get one tooth into the base of my thumb. It was just enough to spring him free. He jumped upward and bit me solidly on top of the head just as help arrived. Kent's mom grabbed the dog chain and my brother grabbed me. He quickly carried me to the back porch. He then put me down. I was now standing there with blood pouring from me like a faucet. I was standing in a pool of it. My clothes were soaked in it. I told my mom, "It is okay. Just put a Band-Aid on it." because I feared a trip to the doctor was in order.

Living far in the country, it would have been a long time waiting for an ambulance in those days, so they simply bundled my head in a towel and put me in the car headed for the hospital. It was a slow and winding 20 mile ride. This gave me time to assess my injuries. My clothes were saturated in blood. My hair was sticky and matted with it. I had bites on my head, one arm, thumb, both legs and buttocks. I had meat hanging out of my leg. The latter was fascinating to an eleven year old, but my mother quickly covered this discovery probably to keep her own sanity. I felt no pain, only stiffness and sleepiness. I talked to my parents the whole way there in order to combat my fears.

When we arrived at the hospital, they waved us straight back through the emergency waiting area and immediately took me to a room. I was intrigued by the way everyone we encountered looked at me. They all seemed a bit pale in my opinion. The first doctor in unwrapped my head and applied a clamp. This was the most pain I had felt all day. It was annoying, like someone pulling your hair really hard nonstop. He then examined each of my wounds and asked the nurse to clean them. This process was painstakingly slow and deliberate, but not painful. She and I chatted the whole time. Next, a gentleman was sent in to shave half of my head. I had never had a shave before and kind of enjoyed the whole experience. The only thing was I was getting tired of laying there. There was, however, more entertainment to come. The nurse returned and proclaimed, "Let's takes that clamp off your head and see if it has stopped bleeding yet!" Sounded good to me. That thing had been pinching me for an hour or more at this point, but when she removed the clamp blood spurted to the ceiling. She was surprised and I was impressed! I then faced a long process of Novocain and stitches over and over again all over my body. The doctor was a kind, gentle man, but it was still not much fun. They debated keeping me overnight for observation, but eventually decided to go ahead and send me home. I was stiff but relieved that the worst appeared to be over. By the time I arrived home, the dog was gone and Kent had moved away.

The next day I awoke very stiff and sore. I walked like an eighty year old. I also began two a day cleansing treatments with peroxide that was aimed at fighting infection. I had each of my wounds scrubbed and cleaned. It was time-consuming work for my mother and an aunt who sometimes stopped to help.

That first day my elementary school principal came to see me. I answered the door, but he acted peculiar simply saying, "I just wanted to see how you were doing," but he did not come in. He was gone in about thirty seconds. I later learned he had been shocked at the sight of me and felt he needed to leave in a hurry. I got a lot of that during that first month. I was a horrible sight. I had about forty stitches in my head in the shape of a question mark as well as in the arms and legs. Half my head was shaved and as the hair grew back, that half was changed from dark brown to blonde due to the constant peroxide treatments.

After about a month, I got the stitches out and was returning to normal. My hair looked funny for a while and I was leery of big dogs, but otherwise, I made it through with only some scars. I have owned many dogs through the years and still love animals in general. As for Kent, he ended up facing a similar fate. The same dog, several months later bit him on the chin. His father did not have the dog destroyed, but instead sold it to an unsuspecting family not disclosing its history. I later learned that the dog had cornered the wife of this family in a basement upon which the husband took a gun and shot the dog.

I have encountered many dog owners over the years who believe that their dog will not hurt anybody when it is clear that their animal poses a threat. I have no tolerance for these people who put others at risk. Ignorance or denial is no excuse when it comes to the well-being of a child.

Bicycle Riding

I ride a bicycle. Not a very common leisure activity for someone in their mid forties. But it is a great hobby. People think riding anywhere from 20-100 miles on a bike is insane. But they fail to realize the joy involved. First, you get to embarrass your children by wearing those tight shorts. It is especially effective to go out for a ride about the time the school bus is coming.

The true value of those funny looking clothes is twofold. Firstly, padding is built in the seat of the biker pants to keep your rear from hurting. It still gets achy on a long ride, but it's at least tolerable. The second reason is that the clothes are tight to keep bugs out, especially the stinging kind. Many beginners learn the hard way when they try to extract an angry wasp from their shirt while doing 40 mph down a hill. The result is often not pretty. That's the same reason I wear sunglasses—to keep the bugs away. Bugs are also often eaten often when you're panting your way up a long hill, swallowed whole to be exact.

I tell everyone how I ride for cardiac health and weight control and all those beneficial things, but my big secret is that it lets me be 12 again. Riding down a long slow slope in the summertime, around dusk when the air begins to cool, surrounded by sweet outdoor aromas, is pure heaven to me. I lean back and forth doing a slow gentle slalom, taking in all the sensations of my senses. The cooling breeze, the scenery passing by, the changing scents and smells as I pass the horse farm and then a grove of pines with their distinctive aroma, followed by a freshly mowed lawn provide ever-changing sensations on my rides.

This feeling takes me back to being a kid because it is something I did many evenings growing up. Peddling to nowhere and back again playing my imaginary games. Now, at my age, I just have to be a little more discreet about pretending I am a glider riding the wind or Evil Knievel getting ready for his big jump. Don't want the neighbors getting any more suspicious about my lack of sanity than they already are.

Bikes are great stress relievers. They use up excess nervous energy and clear your mind. They are a great place to think about everything or about nothing at all. But perhaps the greatest part of a ride for me is the end of a ride. The painful ache of sheer exhaustion is accompanied by a sense of accomplishment. But then it happens. The first fifteen minutes after finishing is spent refreshing myself with water and often sitting in front of a fan. My heart rate begins to slow and my muscles begin to transform from pain to a kind of deep warmth. At this point, my body must release some sort of endorphin, because I gently enter a state of ultimate relaxation and a general feeling of well being. It is better than any high you could ever get from a drug. I am reasonably sure that others who do various forms of exercise feel this too. And it is what keeps you coming back. Exercise is often uncomfortable and even painful at times. But that euphoric feeling you get afterwards is surely a small taste of what heaven must be like.

Mom

Mom, I have a bone to pick with you. And dad too. I mean, you were good parents and all. You raised me well. You taught me right from wrong. You gave me a good moral foundation upon which to live my life. I could not have asked for a better childhood. But where you have failed is in telling me about the things that were to come later in life. You left out some important details that would have been beneficial. Some things I would have preferred to have some prior warning about.

For instance, why would you hide the fact that starting at about age 40, I would have to interrupt my beauty sleep every single night to make a trip to the bathroom? I think this is important stuff. Matter of fact, I consider this to be the main cause of these wrinkles and bags under my eyes. When I was 20, I could sleep uninterrupted for 15 -20 hours and I had no bags or wrinkles. I think if somebody solved this pee problem, they could put a stop to the aging process. And to make matters worse, when I get out of bed to head toward the bathroom, it takes my feet three or four steps to figure out that this is where I am trying to go. They sometimes head toward the kitchen or the living room first. Be honest, is this gonna get worse? You knew this would happen, didn't you? Why did you not warn me?

And what about the doctor's office? You lead me to believe these were nice people. Well I have news for you. These people have means of torture I could not have imagined in my wildest dreams. When I was seven, I worried about getting a shot in the butt. Now I go in for a checkup and usually end up saying something like, "You want to take a what? And put it where?" I have never felt so violated! They ought to be arrested for the stuff they put me through. But you knew this was coming didn't you? I have been through EKG's and ECG's, ABC's and 123's, stress tests, sleep studies, 24 hour monitors strapped to my belly. And I am healthy! What horrible things await me when I actually get something serious? Fess up mom, I know you are holding back.

I base that opinion on the response you gave when I recently called to tell you of my case of vertigo. I had awakened in the middle of the night to the sensation that my bed was flying through the midair and all I had to steer with was my pillow. The room was spinning and I was scared to death. I rushed off to the doctor. They did tests and dispensed drugs to make me happy while I healed. But when I called you to inform you of this incredible experience, you said, quite matter-of-factly, "Yes, I've had that before." MOM! Don't you think you should have mentioned it to me? This would have saved me a lot of trauma. Were you trying to spare me? I am only in my mid 40's. What other surprises are in my future? It is time for you to fess up mom.

Dad, I have to put this one squarely on your lap. You always shaved and groomed yourself in the bathroom with the door closed. I never considered you were hiding the horrors from me. All this hair sprouting from my ears and my back and every other place it shouldn't. I also now know the origin of the phrase "wild hair." I have half a dozen of them in my eyebrows. They grow 43.5 times faster than all the others and they are gray. I fear that if I forget to trim them they may put an eye out. You and mom were always warning me about things that would put my eye out. But I do not recall you ever mentioning eyebrow hair. Why the omission? What else did you leave out?

The list gets longer each year. I sometimes have to grunt to get out of my easy chair. I cannot eat spicy food before bedtime (had to learn that one the hard way too). I pass more and more gas. My jaw clicks when I eat. My pinky joint has a hitch in its giddy up. My teeth are less and less my own. You know, maybe come to think of it, not knowing is a good thing. Based upon what I know so far, the next 50 years might hold horrors so frightening that knowing might separate me from the little sanity I have remaining. Maybe you did the right thing. Maybe, when the time comes, I should keep these secrets from my kids too. WAIT A MINUTE! Now I see! This is a form of revenge isn't it? Payback for all the trouble I caused! Thanks mom and dad! I know what to do now! Hehehe! KIDS!

☞

Why

Why. That is the big question of my life. When you scrape off all the other superficial stuff we fill our lives with, the big question still remains. It does not matter whether you are rich or poor or what you do for a living or what language you speak. I do not even feel it matters whether you are religious or not. At the bottom of it all we still wonder why all of this exists.

By this, I mean us humans, the animals, the plants, the planets, the universe. Some would say that all of the above are creations of God or some higher power. And if that is the case, why does this higher power exist? Why was it created? Did it always exist or did it have a beginning? In either case, why?

The question permeates many parts of our existence. Why are people mean to one another? Why do we feel the need to fight? Why does the earth spin at the speed it does rather than slow down or speed up? Why does it rain every time I get ready to mow the lawn? I did not say all the whys were bad. There are millions of these types of questions. And we attempt to answer many of them with some success.

I guess the core questions though have to do with time and

space and matter. I have struggled with these ones all my life. Not only is it fascinating, but it is for selfish purposes. You see, my number one goal is self preservation. I enjoy existing. And even when times are tough I still prefer it to the alternative.

None of us really know much about tough times. Some have gone through things that threatened to do them in, but most of us are just kind of cruising along. It is not like the sun is burning out next week or we are in the middle of a war zone. We tend to blow up our problems out of proportion and worry about petty stuff.

The big picture questions can at times consume me. I think about how I am so minuscule in the grand scheme of things. My lifetime is barely a spec on the time line of the universe and I am one of the billions of inhabitants on one of the billions of planets. It is very humbling. I know of a few people who need to think a little more often about that.

I do like to think about the past. My body is made up of various base elements. Where were these elements one thousand years ago? Ten thousand? Ten million? What amazing things have parts of my body been witness to? What untold things have I or parts of me been in contact with? That is mind-boggling stuff.

So why am I here? Some will say they are here to find a cure for some disease and while I applaud that endeavor, this will only extend our brief lives by a moment in time. I want a cure for death! Others will say we are here to serve God by many names. Again why? Why does an all-powerful God even piddle with us? If he can control everything about us, then we are kind of like toys, playthings. Atheists say we are here for no reason at all. To them I would ask where did all of this come from then? What set off the Big Bang? I have questions for all factions.

People tend to get angry when you question their beliefs. Most are right fighters. You are either to believe my way or you are wrong. I do not like that tendency. I like to ask questions and play the devil's advocate. I am not trying to be mean. I simply learn a lot from the debate. I think it makes some uncomfortable because they begin to question their own answers.

I have things that happen to which I cannot explain. Personal things upon which I can pin hope for a higher existence. My conscience, that little voice inside me, sometimes gives me unexpected advice or guidance. I find no logical explanation to this. Also, a friend whom I had not seen in years passed away unexpectedly. I have felt a couple of times like they visited my mind just to say things were ok. The funny thing is that the "little voice" had this person's personality and sense of humor. I also had a cat that spent a large portion of my adult life with. When she became terminally ill, she would often have me hold her in a way that she pressed her head against my neck as in a hug. I still feel that sometimes as if she were still a presence.

I am perfectly aware that these things can all be my imagination. That is where faith comes in. Some people believe in those things and some do not. I simply realize that I am too stupid to know which it is.

In a perfect scenario, this existence is simply a type of school of learning environment where we go to be trained in various skills or behaviors. After which we return to the fold on some higher plane where we understand our purpose and feel completed. I think this ending would satisfy any of us.

☞

Pets

Pets play such a large part in out lives. We treat them almost as equal members of the family. Actually, in some cases, they are treated better than some family members. I am sure you know of a case of two where the little dog has bows in its hair and the husband seems to be restrained by a leash and collar. Or how many little old ladies do you know where the house has not one spec of dust, yet you are knocked down by the odor of Fifi's "little accidents" when you walk in the door.

Pets are great consolers when we face strife and insecurity in life. They listen attentively appearing to hang on your every word as you tell them of the dastardly deed that someone victimized you with. You can tell them about the scoundrel who stole your man and you feel as if they feel your pain. But what are they really thinking? Does the cat really care? Or is it just thinking, "I'll lay here as long as you keep scratching my butt, then I'm outta here!" If someone were to go to the kitchen and run the can opener, do you really think the cat would stay and help you dry your tears?

Different personality types talk to their animals in very different ways. We have all seen the baby talkers. They treat two year olds and schnauzers exactly the same. There is of course the gruff, manly type who kinda grunts at his grizzled looking dog and takes pride in how the animal responds on command. Most do communicate in some way with animals and we do hope they at least get the general idea of what we are saying. I have a dog who knows what "go for a ride?" means. She immediately runs toward the car. Does she recognize the words or just the vocal intonations? I am sure someone has done a study about such things using lots of taxpayer dollars, but I have not received a copy of the report yet. Our pets are observant of our actions as well. Just turn on the bathtub faucet and then go out in the other room and try to pet the cat, she will run like the wind. It is mental trauma from a flea bath she once endured. Actually, I was the one suffering most from that experience covered in flea bath and punctures and scratches all about my arms.

Of course there are many nontraditional pets out there as well. Are pet snakes excited when their owner gets home? Are they wondering if you remembered to stop and pick up some fresh mice on your way home? Or do hermit crabs do a little dance when you buy them a roommate? Most of us assign more personality traits to dogs and cats than we do to goldfish. My mother even had a possum at one time. Its mother had been killed in the road by a car and so my mom brought home the baby and raised it. It never seemed to do much but eat and sleep though. Come to think of it, that reminds me of some people I know too.

Larger farm animals are not often called pets, but that is essentially what they are in many cases. You have to be careful, as a kid on a farm, not to get too attached to a critter who will end up on your dinner table next week. Harvey the pig just isn't as easy to chew as the stranger who came from the grocery store. I bet meat consumption would drop dramatically in the cities if people were required to know their dinner before it met its maker. Many people do not associate the meat at the super mart with Bessie the milk cow who stopped producing due to age and was sent to the slaughter house. They do not realize that sometimes you get a steak that is tough as leather because it came from a cow old enough to draw a pension.

Horses are good for those who like bigger pets. The relationship between an animal and its rider is unique. Of course in some parts of the world they ride camels and elephants and such, but on this side of the pond, the horse is king. I cannot imagine what must go through the horses' mind the first time somebody tries to jump on their back. I think once they figure out the program, they think it is kinda cool too. But I feel quite certain in saying I would rather be the first to try to ride a horse than an elephant. I also wonder what pets think of a veterinarian. You take them into the stranger who sits them on a cold slippery table and the first thing he or she does is put a stick in your butt. And things tend to go downhill from there. And you just stand by and let these atrocities happen? No wonder cats split up a hairball on your pillow when you are sleeping. It is called Payback.

An
Odd Interaction

I was witness to an odd interaction the other day—a conversation between two rural, backwoodsy, middle-aged men across the crowded waiting room of a medical clinic. Their sense of decorum and political correctness is quite different from the suburbanites where I live. It created an interesting encounter of which I was not particularly shocked, since I grew up in Appalachia, but to many not from that background I am certain it would have been downright shocking.

Larry spoke first to George, "Haven't seen you in a while."

"Yep! Been a couple years. You still down on the crick?" responded George.

"Um hmm. They are stockin' trout up my way this afternoon. I was in water up to my neck yesterday tryin' to tie off a tree before they come."

Larry said. "Your brother still in prison?"

"Naw, he got out and moved to Templeton," George stated very matter-of-factly. "Heard your brother had cancer. Is he still sick?"

"They cut it out and he is back workin' now." Larry said.

The people in the waiting room took this all in intently but with no appearance of shock or dismay. The conversation was right out there for all to hear. Being a small community, most everybody there probably knew all of the involved parties. Even more impressive was the fact that either of these men considered the conversation to be intrusive. It was as if they were discussing the price of bread.

The candid nature of their talk was quite a refreshing thing. There was no malice and certainly no putting on or faking. These country folks are real and true and you can rely upon their word. The rest of us could probably learn a lot from them.

Porches

One of the things I miss most from my childhood that I no longer have in my life is a house with a big porch. Like most homes today, my porch is about the depth of a postage stamp, barely big enough to put a couple chairs out there.

My grandfather had a great porch. It was probably 10'x15' and indented into the corner of the house in such a way that it had two walls with doors leading into the kitchen or the living room. The other two sides had wooden banisters around them. These were 3 foot high wooden "half walls" that were probably 12" wide so you could even sit on top of them if you wanted. The open areas were flanked by two large shady trees creating a cool and private environment. Yet there was still enough openness to see the road and wave at passers by.

The porch had a plank wooden floor and two creaky screen doors. No porch is complete without at least one screen door with a squeaky spring.

There was a large wooden rocking chair and a big wooden swing suspended by chains from the ceiling. The benefits of this porch as a kid were that it allowed ample room to play outside even when the weather was bad. It was a great place to spend a rainy day well protected from the elements. Porches served a very useful purpose. In those days, nobody in our area had air conditioning. The porch was an evening escape from the summer heat which seemed to linger inside the house late into the evening. It also created more socialization between neighbors. You would wave at or chat with passers by.

I had a great-uncle who had a porch that went around three sides of his house. That was my idea of a porch! You and your parents could be on the porch at the same time and they still could not see you doing things you shouldn't. That uncle was a lifelong bachelor, so I am not sure why he needed so much porch, but I was still envious.

The porch on my parent's house was set up like my grandfather's with two walls and banisters. It was not as spacious as his, but it was still a good place to hang out. My father later framed it in and turned it into a sunroom. He has done a lot of things right in his life but that was not one of them. I missed the porch.

Porches of any size to be useful have largely been replaced by decks on newer houses. But I find these to be worthless. They provide no shade from the sun. The floor is even hot to your bare feet. It is not protection from the rain. It has no place to hang a good swing. And it is only useful after the sun has gone down. I feel this idea has been pushed on the public because it is cheaper to build, but it does not make it better. Progress is not always a step forward.

If I am ever rich enough to build a custom house, you'd better believe it will have a big deep porch with a swing and a squeaky screen door. If it does not squeak, I am taking it back to the store.

Little Decisions, Big Results

There are many decisions we make in life every day. Mostly mundane with little true significance as to how our lives are to commence from this point. Yet there are on rare occasions those seemingly insignificant decisions which can alter the course of your entire future. The only thing is at the time you have no idea how profound the choices you make will become.

I have recently experienced just such a circumstance. Those seemingly simple moments have culminated into massive changes which I believe will have a lasting and positive effect on the remaining years of my life, all 350 of them.

It has taken me 40+ years to figure out what I truly want out of life. It has been a true learning experience. And while I am far from at the end of my search for self, I certainly feel I have a better grip on it than at any point in the past. I also have come to the understanding that I must actively pursue the kind of life I want. Passivity creates doubt and indecision. I have learned that throughout life, my greatest moments were when I followed my own heart and intuition and just got the job done, whatever it was. Sure I have had failures as well, but the successes have made them all worthwhile.

Taking control of my own circumstances has been harder than it would appear on the surface. We are all so conditioned to lead a life to the specifications of society at large. But as unique beings I do not feel we should all fit into the same mold. It stifles our individual creativity. I no longer desire to live my life for the pleasing of everyone else. I can honestly say that if I am living to the satisfaction of my own conscience and fulfilling the desires of my own heart in a positive manner, then that is all that really matters.

PB-n-P

There are few things in life more enjoyable than a home cooked meal. The satisfaction in preparing and consuming a family favorite is hard to match. In the old days this was a normal part of everyday life, but now with the convenience and fast foods and bust lifestyles, the home cooked family meal is more of a rarity.

We are having a family meal tonight of homemade chili and rolls and a special dessert made by my 11 year old daughter. My children have taken and interest in helping cook over the past few years and they seem to be getting very good at it. This will serve them well in life, talent they can always use, and maybe, like for me, a hobby to enjoy.

Cooking has a history of utilitarian purposes and while that part may be fading with the growing market of convenience foods, the creativity and style of cooking will always be a passion for some of us. We all have a different way of doing it and different ideas about what is good, but being able to envision a dish and then bring it to life is a special talent that not everyone possesses.

A great meal can be as simple as grilled burgers and fries to an elaborate array of ingredients blended into a gourmet meal of great splendor. To me the two best kinds of cooks are those who can improve upon a traditional dish, or the ones who can create completely new taste sensations. These are the innovators of our diets. You wonder where in the world they ever got the idea. The origins of some of these dietary wonders would surely make for an interesting story. Some that pique my curiosities are:

Peanut butter on celery
Pineapple on Ham
Gravy on French Fries
Chili on just about anything

The list could be endless. What are your favorite oddball combinations? No wonder we all are getting fatter. One of my most misunderstood snacks is the peanut butter and pickle sandwich. I was first introduced to this marvel of culinary genius at about the age of four by Roy, my babysitter's husband. He was a cheerful, energetic, slight fellow who loved kids and loved to do little things to make their world special. So I enjoyed spending time with him. He was a kid kind of guy. A carpenter by trade, he was always building and fixing things and being his helper was one of my favorite ways to spend an afternoon. Even though I was probably more trouble to him than I was worth, he never complained once.

I do not know if Roy invented the peanut butter and pickle sandwich of whether it was simply a secret family recipe passed down from generation to generation, but either way, I am glad he felt he could share it with me. It is as it sounds, peanut butter (creamy not crunchy) and sliced pickles (dill not sweet) slathered between two slices of bread. People who do not have an open mind to new experiences for the pallet cringe at the mere mention of it. But those of us with the courage to explore new horizons find the combination to be a lifelong love affair. Even among my own three children, only one of them has the refined taste buds necessary to appreciate such a delicacy. She and I relish in our oral pleasure while the rest of the family looks at us like we are nuts.

The reason this is on my mind is because just recently I ran into Roy after not having seen him in many years. He was now an old fellow, but still sporting that winning smile and cheerful disposition. I told him how much I had enjoyed the time I spent with him as a child and how I still ate his wonderful concoction regularly. He smiled with that gleam in his eye and said that he too still had about one per week. I then introduced my daughter and let him know that his legacy lives on. That was a proud moment for me.

I also now know that many who read this will now be trying this long held secret and before you know it there will be fast food PBnP's in every town and then they will surely follow with gourmet Peanut butter and Pickle salons where you can get your organically grown peanuts hand crushed and mixed with a virgin custom oil and then combined with your choice of 132 pickle varieties on any of 17 different breads or rolls. They will even have a low carb version!

So go ahead, sneak on into the kitchen right now and discover what you have been missing all these years. You know you want to!

Pap

Pap was a character. Unique in so many ways. In his 86 years he never traveled more than probably 150 miles from where he was born. He reluctantly embraced only the most basic of modern conveniences. At least he had a radio and he really seemed to enjoy reading the local newspaper almost cover to cover in the evenings. And when he would spend an occasional evening at our house, he would watch a little television, though he would never let on that it was even the least bit tempting to him.

His home was old. It was not equipped with indoor plumbing. Someone had purchased parts to install a toilet and bathroom sink at some point, but that was as far as it ever went. He was content with the outhouse around in the backyard or the bucket on the steps he used as an alternative on cold winter nights.

Water for drinking, bathing, and cleansing was drawn by a hand pump sitting on well in the side yard about ten feet off the front porch. This pump had to be primed. This was done by pouring about a quart of leftover water into the top of this contraption and then vigorously pumping the handle until water began to pour from a spout which you gathered into a bucket carried to the house. Needless to say, a "bath" was normally a wash rag in a basin.

Pap had a farm. A plot of 175 rough, hilly acres that he cared for and tended every day. He raised beef cows. His favorites were Herefords. The secret everyone knew was that these animals were really his pets. They were the fattest cows for miles around. And you just knew that deep inside he hated ever sending one to market to be sold. They were his best friends with whom he spent his days. The farm was a couple of miles out the blacktop ridge road from his house. He had originally lived on the farm until the little house there could no longer sustain his family. So at some point, they had moved to his current residence abandoning the old farmhouse to be used for hay storage.

He went to the farm every morning about daylight and stayed until 5pm or so. To hear him tell it, he would be hard at work all day, but we would get quite a chuckle out of sneaking up on him sleeping on the porch of the old house. I think he had a good nap every afternoon. That was his heaven on earth. Relaxing on the porch of that old dilapidated house with the cows grazing on what was once the yard.

Up until the very last few years, all his farming was done with two work horses named Fanny and Nell. They were used for heavy duty work around the farm such as plowing the gardens and hauling hay on a hay sled. The hay was put up loose, stacked into haystacks several feet tall. The work was hard and hot in the summer, bone chilling cold in the winter. Modern conveniences like a tractor and a hay bailer would have lightened the load considerably. But Pap would have considered that surrendering to laziness. He kept the areas around the lane and along the edges of the field trimmed with a scythe. Everything was done in a deliberate, old-fashioned manner.

The animals and people both were supplied water at the farm by a spring. A kind of pool that had been dug out and then a shack constructed over it to collect the water. From there, a pipe ran down to a 55-gallon steel drum into which the water constantly flowed. The excess simply ran over the edge. The end of the pipe is where people got their drink. The animals drank from the drum. So simplistic in its design, yet so effective. And on a 90-degree day when all covered in sweat and hayseeds, that water was like nectar from the Gods. So cold and refreshing, nothing could have been sweeter.

Pap lived alone his last twenty years or so. His beloved wife had departed in her sleep in her early sixties. He had three children. One had been killed in an accident at his job and the other two, one son and one daughter, were married with their own families. As you might imagine, he was not much of a homemaker. His house had three upstairs bedrooms as I recall, an unfinished cellar for storage and the main floor had a kitchen, dining room and living room. The living room and bedrooms were never used. He had simply shut off that part of the house, probably to hide from the pain of its memories. His wife, Bessie, had passed in 1960 and at that time a few old timers still had funerals in their homes. So the last major use of the living room had been as a funeral parlor. I think that was simply too much for him to bear.

The small kitchen had a gas cooking stove, a sink basin, a china cabinet, and a kitchen table. All were stacked full of the necessities of life. He was not a cook by any means. He ate cereal for breakfast, took a sandwich to the farm for lunch, and then his daughter brought his dinner to him each night from the leftovers of her family's meal. She was always met with the proclamation. "Jesus Christ! There's enough food there for ten men! " But the next day you could find no signs of any leftovers.

The dining room had been named due to its original purpose. But in its current arrangement it contained a refrigerator, tow large wooden rocking chairs, a chest of drawers, a gas heating stove and a rollaway bed upon which Pap slept. Three beds upstairs, one very fit man, yet he chose the rollaway. Pap shared his home with an animal too. At first Tiny, was a Chihuahua. She was a little chubby thing with a hoarse bark who would snap at you if she was not happy with how things were going. Upon her passing, he inherited Patches. She was a quiet lap loving cat who would long outlive Pap. I think he enjoyed the evenings spent in the rocking chair or on the front porch swing with his miniature companions. So long as nobody knew they were on his lap.

Pap's life was full and vibrant up until about eighteen months before his demise when his aging heart began failing him in sputters and spurts. He suffered from congestive heart failure. This meant he had good days and not so good ones. He would have difficulty remembering things and would often get confused. His daughter provided the hands on care and he was in and out of the hospital on a regular basis. The worst part for him was the loss of that little piece of heaven that had sustained him for so many years. He now had to rely on others to do the chores around the farm and they never did them quite up to his standards. Or they would use a machine where he thought a strong back would do just fine. His diminishing abilities and reliance on others were a great burden on such an independent spirit. He never really adjusted to this new reality. When his time came to go, I think he knew it. And I think he felt the time was probably right as the world he so loved was changing into something he could no longer understand. He was not one of the last of a bygone era when he left this world in 1986. Not that long ago, yet his reality and that of many people today were a million miles apart.

Valentine's
Day

Valentine's Day is almost here. Who the heck came up with this holiday anyway? There are so many potentially bad scenarios for this one that a guy feels like he is trapped in the middle of a minefield.

Firstly, you could simply forget it was Valentine's Day. "Oops, slipped my mind! Is it February already?"

That'll cost you more in misery than you can possibly bear. You could also make the mistake of giving her a smaller bouquet or box of chocolates than the other girls at her office received. Again, you will pay in many ways for your sins. You can give her the wrong color.

"You know I do not like yellow roses! Or at least you should!" she would say, digging your grave deeper.

The worst thing though may be if you buy the wrong size in something to wear. Avoiding clothing all together can save you from hearing, "You think I'm fat don't you?" or "Do you think I look that big?" Trouble all around!

Of course even if you do luck up and get the right candy, the right flowers, and the right nightie, it will all end up as trouble. Because after eating that five-pound box of chocolates, that darned underwear is not gonna fit anymore after all and it will be your fault!

Cross
Country

Two weeks ago was the beginning of cross country practice at Shelly's middle school. She had decided many months ago that this was something she wanted to try. Through the spring, she had gone jogging to get into better running condition. Although the summer's heat eventually put a stop to that, I felt she was prepared enough that she could get through the first few practices without feeling totally overwhelmed.

The first practice was a hot humid day. They ran three-quarters of a mile. Shelly came home without much to say about it. The next day was a half-mile and, being typical August weather, still 90 degrees and humid. This was tough weather to start. She still had little to say. The third day was yet another one-half mile but this time she came home and let her frustrations out.

"Mindy keeps beating me!" she confessed. "And I am always almost last."

Mindy was a good friend with whom Shelly spent considerable time. Mindy was really into horses and Shelly sometimes went over to help in their grooming. They would have sleep overs and go various places together. All in all they were good friends.

Mindy was the type that did not like to lose at anything. She was also the type that would never admit to this shortcoming. She was an only child and suffered from center of attention syndrome. She was not a bad kid or a mean kid or anything like that, but you just saw a slight jealous streak in her when the spotlight passed her by.

She was also new to this cross country thing. And although she was no match for the more seasoned runners, if she could just beat Shelly every day, that would pacify her ego. She had convinced Shelly that the best way to get through this grueling ordeal was to run fast then walk a while. They would do this over and over again until they got close to the finish where Mindy knew she could beat Shelly in a final sprint. She was controlling the parameters in order to suit her abilities.

Now that Shelly had made me aware of her difficulties, I knew I could help her. I had run cross country in high school. I was not very good at it, but I understood the concept. I explained to her about pacing, how slow and steady wins the race. I told her to follow my plan and she would be leaving Mindy in the dust in no time. It was nothing personal. I like Mindy just fine. But this was a battle for Shelly's self esteem!

I told her the first day to pick out someone whom she knew ran slow, but never walked, and follow them. No matter what position they were in, follow them everywhere. Shelly thought I was nuts. Why should everybody else, including Mindy, get a head start like that? I insisted that my plan would work so she relented and agreed to try my plan.

That evening Shelly told me of how she had followed some poor girl all around the course. She laughed about how the girl got kind of paranoid about it. She told me of how they were in dead last for the first half of the run but then slowly began passing one runner after another. She talked of how with each pass she felt more energized and encouraged to plow forward, and how in the end, she had finished in the middle of the pack. She was greatly encouraged. However, Mindy had still finished ahead of her. I explained that if she stuck with my plan, Mindy's time was coming.

Now that the threshold had been broken, I explained that there was no turning back. Never again was Shelly to walk on the course. I explained that she should keep running when Mindy walked. And when Mindy began to run again, Shelly should pick up the pace a bit making it more difficult for Mindy to catch up. This way Mindy would be tired by the time she caught up and would feel the need to walk some more.

The next day Shelly returned home smiling. Mindy had still beat her, but she had been very stressed to do so. Shelly said that Mindy kept asking if she was ready to walk some. Shelly would just bark "No!" and keep running. She could see the frustration on Mindy's face. I told Shelly that she was getting faster each day and that Mindy could not continue to walk and expect to catch up with her sprints. She was beginning to see the light.

Sure enough the very next day it happened. Shelly came home and proclaimed "I DID IT!" She explained how Mindy had struggled mightily just to catch back up in her sprints and as soon as she was in earshot would plead with Shelly asking if she was ready to walk now. Shelly would simply say "Nope!" and keep running. She must have broken Mindy's spirit in the end because she beat her by a solid forty seconds! Shelly was also now in the top third of all the runners.

Last night I worked with Shelly on her stride. She was using what I call a tired runner's shuffle. I showed her how to extend that stride and make her effort more efficient. She is like putty for me now. I can mold her into a really good runner. And she is looking forward. Mindy is conquered. Her next target is Celeste. The girl who always finishes first! Look out Celeste! Shelly's sneaking up behind you!

And It Didn't
Cost a Thing

We all know that 99% of us are much too materialistic. We want the latest gadgets, gizmos, styles and trends. And we will pay a premium to get it. But when you think about your greatest memories and moments in your own life, do those things even play a role in the things that you remember most?

My own personal favorite memories are from things that might be considered small and insignificant and most of all were often free. My father used to take me on a hike about once per year usually on a Saturday in the fall down an old abandoned road that was no longer used. It was a trek through the woods from a ridge down into a valley of probably two miles each way. We would see all sorts of critters, squirrels, chipmunks, deer, ruffed grouse, pheasants, etc. ... It was a nice way to get in touch with nature. But the thing I enjoyed the most was getting to swing on the grapevines.

Wild grapevines crisscrossed the woods in the area I grew up. They would dangle from tree branches high up in the canopy. The key was to find one at the edge of a ravine that was far enough from the main trunks of any trees. You would then test its strength to be sure it was attached well before cutting it at about three feet above the ground. Typically these were two to three inches in diameter and very woody in texture so the cutting took a couple of minutes. Once you had the cut complete, the only thing left to do was grab hold of the vine, take a few steps backward, let out your best Tarzan yell, then lift your feet and fly. I would sail out over the ravine, the ground moving further from my feet with a big grin on my face. Upon reaching the apex of my flight, the vine would return me to the spot I had begun. If the planning had been done properly, no tree trunks were encountered in my flight path. I would repeat this over and over again for the better part of an hour before getting tired. We would then settle down to eat peanut butter and jelly sandwiches before continuing on our journey.

My father also once told me a story about swinging on the vines from when he was a kid. He said that he and his next older brother were out playing in the woods when they found a vine that would take them way out over a steep slope. So they cut it and began to swing. It was at such a spot that at the top of your swing the ground had dropped away a good 30 feet or so. The problem was that one of his much younger brothers had tagged along on this trip and was relentlessly bugging the older ones for his turn. Several times they told him that he was simply too young to ride this particular vine, but of course he thought they were just being selfish with all the fun. So of course he thought they were just being selfish with all the fun. So as kids often do, they grew tired of his whining and gave in to his demands and let him have a turn. With much joy and satisfaction he took the vine, backed up as far as his little feet would take him and away he flew. My dad said the last thing they heard him say as he reached the farthest point of his swing was "I can't hang on!" They would have sworn that he was dead and what in the world they tell their mother, but after climbing down the hill they found him dazed and confused but otherwise unhurt and asking if he could go again.

My father was also responsible for another of my favorite memories. There was a large pond in a neighbor's cow pasture up the road that was manmade and intentionally not very deep, maybe two feet or so. It was a summer watering hole for the cows and a winter ice-skating rink for every kid within miles. We would play hockey and tag and build a fire to keep warm and roast marsh-mallows. It was a great place.

My father had grown up ice skating on creeks and streams and was quite good at it. But he was now in his mid 50's and had not skated in years. But one Sunday morning when there was nobody else at the pond, he took me skating, just me and my dad skating on that pond for an hour or so. He showed me how to do some tricks. I am sure it was good for him too. I bet he felt like a kid again. But that simple hour of free fun will always be one of my best memories.

My mother was often the victim of out practical jokes. We would do all sorts of things to torment her as she was such a good target. But the best one was not of our doing, but was conceived by a monkey. We were visiting a smallish amusement park that had a zoo. My mother has always loved animals, so of course she would not miss the opportunity to visit them. On this particular day she was captivated by a particular monkey. He was in a cage with some other monkeys and she was trying to make small talk with him, kind of like you talk to a baby. The monkey retreated to the far side of the cage to get a drink of water but quickly returned to where my mother was standing. Then all of the sudden he sprayed her with the water which he was still holding in his mouth. She was soaked. Everybody around got a big kick out of that one.

My best friend and I were on the elementary school play-ground one Saturday playing tennis. On one end of the tennis court just past the fence was a long hill which went on for prob-ably 50 yards with a creek running along the bottom. On the other side of the creek was a cow pasture surrounded by a wire fence. We had hit a couple of balls over the fence by accident and gad gone down the hill to retrieve them when Curt spotted a kickball on the other side of the creek.

This was early March and the water was much too cold for wading. The creek was too wide for jumping. But that ball looked so tempting, too good to just leave there. Then my friend had an AHA moment. There was a point upstream where the fence di-agonally cut across the creek. It was a very long span, but if he was careful, he could get across the creek. It was a very long span, but if he was careful, he could get across, retrieve the ball and then climb back. There was little I could do to help so I just sat down in the grass to enjoy the show.

From my vantage point I could see the top half of the fence and the creek banks but not the water itself. My friend went up to the point where the fence started across and climbed on moving slowly toward the middle. Since this was such a long span be-tween fenceposts, it was kind of wobbly. As he reached the middle, the fence began to sway back and forth harder and harder as my friend tried to regain balance and control. But in the end the fence won. It flipped backward violently one last time extracting him from his tenative hold. About a second later the first inevitable splash came up. I would have gone to help him but I was laughing too hard to even stand. He gathered himself from the frigid water and made the quickest 2-mile trip home to get in front of the fire I have ever seen.

There are many stories from my life that I cherish and most of them were spontaneous and/or free. So do not burden yourself with too much in the way of material possessions instead and take a full helping of the little moments that make a life rich and full.

The Musician
in Me

I grew up playing music on a stage in front of a crowd. It started in the fourth grade when the band director came around and introduced us to various instruments and told us we could learn to play them if we could convince our parents to spend a little money. I wanted to play the drums.

The band teacher was a short, quiet woman who was attentive to details. She taught me the basic rudiments and encouraged me to reach for my potential. I was hooked. Within six months I had moved from a drum pad all the way to a full drum set. I practiced frequently and enjoyed making music.

My father, as it happened, played what I would term mountain music or old style country/bluegrass. He was encouraging of my interest in music and before long I was practicing with his band. He knew the best way to learn was by simply doing. So it was not long before I was playing my first public gig at a dance with his band. This vocation was the centerpiece of my life for the next twenty years. Being so young, people were instantly praising my talents and showering me with compliments. That was simply fuel to the fire.

At first I was playing maybe two or three nights a month but that soon grew. As time went on, it became every week. By age fifteen I had expanded to playing night club bands as well. I was very busy. I also was making excellent spending money for a kid. I continued to expand my musical endeavors as I grew up and ended up making a large part of my living at it through most of my twenties.

We have all seen bands play and enjoyed being entertained. But what most people do not know what goes on from the musician's point of view. Of course all musicians enjoy the praise and compliments, the fans, the prestige of sorts from those who look up to you. It is also fun to be able to use your creative energies in such a manner. But what I miss that most people would not realize is the voyeuristic nature of the job.

Most songs you play become almost second nature. They do not require your full conscious attention. So to entertain yourself you end up watching the crowd. You watch the dancers good and bad. You see people apply alcohol to the point where they invent dance moves never seen before and hopefully never seen again. You see poor blokes impishly make their way across the floor to ask some stranger to dance only to have to turn and retreat with their tail between their legs. You see others who began the night as strangers ending the night as the best of friends as well as some who come together and leave apart. There is much to be learned about relationships in a nightclub.

Being a musician is also a job where it is difficult to call in sick or worse yet, be late or go home early. How do you tell five hundred partygoers "Sorry, I think I am coming down with something. Gonna use half a sick day. Bye!" I remember being so sick I would go lay down and groan between sets, then I would put my smile back on and go out and perform my heart out. Can you imagine playing drums with a bad headache? They do not make painkillers strong enough for that which allow you to remain conscious.

A band is a marriage between four to six people. You live, eat and sleep together. It can be tremendously rewarding, but also trying. Difficulty in blending all those personalities is the most common reason for bands not succeeding. You get to travel and see things that most people only dream about and it is part of your job. People put you on a pedestal and give you all sorts of special treatment.

Performing music can force you to grow as a person by putting you in situations where you must overcome fear or lack of confidence in order to succeed. I faced just such a situation when I took a brief stint as a soloist for a Christmas show in Nashville. My part was to play guitar and sing in the round surrounded by a crowd on both my level and a balcony level above. The crowd was very close and people were everywhere, above and all around. Just me, my guitar, and a microphone, there was nowhere to hide a mistake, and in a city where music is done at the highest level of quality. Every pluck, every utterance had to be right. Kind of like those figure skaters on television, the pressure was on. But the rush you feel when it is over and you have done it right is addictive. You begin to search for more and more ways to reignite that feeling. Playing to a live audience was my greatest love.

Studio work was a whole different kind of adventure. In the old days they simply played a song over and over again until they got it right, but technology changed all that. Now you play it through then go back and fix it a word or phrase at a time. Kinda funny to stand there and sing one or two words then the technician simply plugs it in the right spot replacing the sour notes you sang the first time through.

The first time I played drums in a studio was depressing. They took me into a room all by myself and closed the door. Made me feel like an outcast. They only talked to me through a headset I was wearing. I began to feel self conscious. Smelling my armpits and checking my teeth in the mirror for foreign objects. What did I do wrong? Why couldn't I play with the others? The reason turned out to be that they did not want the drums "bleeding" sound into the other microphones. They could control mixing sound levels better this way. I ended up doing many studio sessions over the years but it was never as good as a crowd.

Eventually the time came for me to stop playing music, grow up and get a real job. Well, at least I have accomplished the first one. But I will always be grateful for the opportunities and experiences my music gave me. Whether you play for the world or just for yourself, I believe everyone should try it. It can be a great form of self therapy and a creative outlet. It soothes the soul. It does not matter whether anyone else enjoys your songs as long as you do.

Beware
of Fork

If I were to list the five most significant and/or memorable bodily injuries I have sustained in my life, one of the items on the list would read, "Fork Incident." In all my years, I have rarely been more perplexed when attempting to understand how something happened than I am with this particular event.

I must have been eight or nine at the time. I was in elementary school. Each day I would get home at around 3:45 or so. My mother would already be home from work by then and my father was usually just arriving about the same time as my bus. We would all be hungry about this time, so we often ate supper at around 4:15 or 4:30.

We were not formal at all in our eating arrangements. Mom would simply make up plates and send us on our way. Unlike today, homes back then only had one television in them. Ours was a portable 19" black and white Admiral. There were no big screens, or remotes or 10,000 channels. We had three, maybe four on a good day. And as barbaric as it may seem, we had to walk across the room to change the channel dial.

Like most kids, I loved to watch television while eating my supper. Also, like most kids, I had a lazy streak in me. Therefore I had developed a way to get all I needed from the kitchen to the living room in one trip. I would take a chair from the kitchen table and place upon it my dinner plate, my drink and my silverware. Then I would carefully carry the whole mess to the living room. Sure there were other chairs in there, but none of them was close enough to the television to suit me. I wanted to be so close that mom would have to warn me that I was gonna go blind watching that thing from way up there.

I had made this journey a habit for quite some time and this day was nothing out of the ordinary. I had turned on the television and then went to the kitchen to get my chair. I got a can of pop and mom gave me my plate and silverware. I loaded it all on the chair and began my slow, meticulous journey to the living room. I carried the chair, holding it by the seat, about waist high. My path took me across one end of the dining room which was constructed of knotty pine walls and floors. As I was making my way, my fork began to slide off the edge of the chair. This did not really concern me much, I could return to retrieve it once I had delivered my cargo. Besides what harm could a little floor dirt on it do to an eight year old?

Then it happened. The fork fell to the floor. It then bounced back up traveling past the chair seat clear up to my head, miraculously with enough force to lodge itself vertically between my right eyeball and temple. What a fine mess I had gotten myself into. I could just sense that this was gonna keep me from watching the after-school special. The fork was stuck in there good too. No way I could hide this one. It didn't really hurt but I was gonna need some help.

I reluctantly returned to the kitchen where my mom was rinsing out something in the sink. I walked over to her and said, "Mom, can you pull this fork out of my head?"

My mother turned to me, muttered something like "My God!" and then yanked the fork right out of my head leaving four little puncture holes there.

After a brief discussion with my father, they decided a trip to the emergency room was in order. So down the road we went the twenty miles or so to town. I was in no pain. It was just four little holes. This trip ought to be a piece of cake. I just wish the doctors and nurses had seen it my way. Upon arrival, they proceeded to prod and poke and pour every burning, boiling substance known to man in those holes. They talked about infections and possible internal damage and precautionary measures. All I knew was that the treatment was much worse than the injury.

In the end everything checked out fine. I had been a lucky young man. If the fork had landed a half inch further left, I would have lost an eye, half an inch further right and it would have entered my temple. But the question that has haunted me all these years is how in the world did a fork fall two feet from the chair to the floor and then rebound four feet upward with such a force that it planted itself firmly in my head? Did my brother have something to do with it? Or maybe it was that evil girl who lived up the street ... she always had it in for me. Maybe it was my magnetic personality. The possibilities are endless. But heed my warning and never turn your back on your fork. It may be out to get you.

☞

R and R
in a Hospital Bed

My father is eighty-seven and a half years old and after a long, fruitful, productive life, he is now plagued with many of the same ailments which await us all if we stick around long enough.

It all started about three months ago when he was outside tinkering around with the work he dearly loves. He was attempting to attach a trailer to the back of his tractor when his foot slipped and he was quickly deposited rear end first onto the pavement. The accident, while painful, was hardly considered serious at the time, just a sore tail bone. He had done much worse in his life as a farmer and factory laborer. However, the soreness that followed turned into a stabbing pain that within a week made walking prohibitive. This cause of inactivity then led to pneumonia and the pneumonia led to successive hospital stays where he contracted a staph infection.

This progression weakened his will, his spirit, and his body and created a circumstance where it became uncertain at times whether he would live or die both in his own mind as well as in the minds of his family and his caregivers.

His present hospital stay has dragged out to about a month so far, and though these past few days have shown improvement and stability, I remain aware that his fortunes can turn on a dime. His daily routine has been altered to an endlessly repeating cycle of doctors, nurses, and therapists. It is dizzying and overwhelming.

He is awakened each morning at around six o'clock for a finger stick to check his blood sugar level. This has been made necessary by a steroid he has been taking to clear his lungs which has a side effect of raising his sugar level dramatically. He is then allowed to fall back to sleep for twenty minutes or so until the respiratory therapist arrives. This person comes by four times a day, disconnects his oxygen tube, and replaces it with a mask through which my father must inhale a foggy chemical concoction for seven minutes.

Next, following another thirty-five minutes of blissful slumber, the student nurse arrives for his morning bathing. Dad is encouraged to do as much as possible on his own with assistance. Breakfast soon follows at seven thirty. In the middle of breakfast another nurse enters with the morning pills. A paper cup filled with a dozen little manmade miracles designed to cure his ills. Also, in this time period, the cafeteria lady arrives to recite dad's lunch options. As he sits there picking through his morning eggs, he is asked to weigh the benefits of chicken vs tuna salad and pears vs peaches.

As the last bites of breakfast are thrown back across the tongue, the swallow lady stops by and in her ever cheerful manner says she needs to watch him drink to determine if a thickening agent is still needed in dad's beverages.

Business is picking up! The nurse is back to take vitals. The cafeteria lady is back for the breakfast tray. The physical therapist is checking in to see if dad is ready to do some arm and leg exercises and the occupational therapist wants him to stand up and play poker!

Are you kidding me? It is only 9:30am and I am already worn out just from watching! So much for rest and relaxation!

Against
All Odds

Eric grew up in the 1960's and 1970's in rural mid-America. He was a typical kid in many ways. He was however blessed with above average intelligence and excelled in school. Friends were plentiful and enemies few. He had a personality that fit in with most crowds. His way with people would be a lifelong asset. Eric enjoyed sports but there were no organized leagues in rural America at that time below high school level and even few at that point. So the competition was limited to neighborhood pickup games that were sometimes arranged as well as gym class at school. What you learned about the games was merely by trial and error as no formal coaching was available.

Eric did learn along the way that the churches of his area had a men's softball league in which many of the athletic types competed. The minimum allowed was 13 but most participants were 18-30 years old. Rarely did you see any 16-year-olds and never a 13-year-old player. But Eric was anxious to try. He wanted to be involved and play with the "big boys."

When he was 11 or 12, he began to hang around his local

team's practices. He would retrieve foul balls and play catch with the odd man out during warm-ups. He was just always around. This familiarity made him friends with some of the team. He slowly grew into roles. He would field balls in the outfield when they were shorthanded during practice. He also would hit practice grounders and pop flies to the fielders. He was beginning to fit in. That personality was making him a part of the crowd.

A defining moment came when he was twelve. He was filling in at third base during batting practice for the team. This was a "hot" position on a team due to the closeness to the batter as well as the long throw to first base for ground outs. But this was just warm-ups, nothing was expected of him but to retrieve balls.

The team was about halfway through batting practice when Johnny Hicks came to bat. He was known for being a good contact hitter and fastest man on the team. He was a very friendly type and one of Eric's best buddies on the team. Johnny was about 20. He had made a few swings scattering balls around the outfield. The next pitch came in belt high and on the inside part of the plate. Johnny's eyes lit up. This was in his wheelhouse. He let it rip. A line drive hard down the third base line right at Eric! This was as hard as a ball could be hit and he was only sixty feet away!

Eric had only a split second to react and only two choices flashed through his mind. Catch it or die! Up went his glove to chest high. The ball smacked his glove with incredible force and he managed to squeeze it shut through the excruciating pain. To remove his attention from himself and the pain, he immediately took the ball from his glove with his right hand and fired a perfect strike to the first baseman! The players were impressed. They thought for sure he was gonna be injured but instead he had executed a perfect mock double play! Eric never let on about the pain and fortunately no other balls of consequence were catapulted at his throbbing hand that day.

The seed had been planted. The obstacles removed. The next spring at age 13 years and 4 months, Eric showed up at tryouts and made the team. He had been given this rare chance based upon his perseverance over the previous years. Among the grownups, he was an average player, but he held his own. Excellent for a mere kid. He was young and fast and a good outfielder. His fleet feet got him some base hits where others would not have made it. But his worth to the team would soon be realized.

The team as a whole was excellent. They were undefeated through the season. They were blessed with some wonderfully gifted players. Eric felt fortunate to just be on the team. He was playing about half the time, usually in center field. He was steady, consistent.

The playoffs came and the competition became more fierce. The team faced some close games, but managed to continue sneaking through. They had reached the league championship game. Eric felt fortunate just to be on a team, but to be playing for the league championship? Could it get any better than this?

The game went on pretty typically for a contest of two talented teams. A lone run here or there. Eric was on the bench. The games were seven innings and in the top of the seventh with the score tied 2-2, Eric was sent in to pinch run for one of the older guys who had gotten a lead off hit. It was hoped that his speed would help to manufacture a run. The next batter popped out. Eric remained stranded at first. The following batter got a single to right field and Eric was on the move. With the coach waiving him onward, he trotted into third safely. Runners were now on first and third with one out. Now his heart was pounding. As the next batter stepped in, he could envision an impending collision on a play at the plate. That catcher was huge! Eric wondered how he could ever get past him.

The truth turned out to be less climatic. The batter hit a long fly allowing Eric to tag up and trot safely home for the go ahead run. Eric felt overwhelming joy at being a part of this. The inning ended with a final ground out and a 3-2 advantage. They were three outs from the title. Three simple outs! No big deal!

Eric now took the field to play center fielder. It was where he was most comfortable. The action began early in the bottom of the inning with a single up the middle. Eric was up quickly and fired the ball to the infield holding the runner. Another hit to right. It was now first and second with nobody out. All of the sudden the euphoria was being replaced with incredible tension. The momentum was swinging back to the opposition.

The next batter hit a lazy pop fly to the catcher. No damage. This was followed by a slow grounder toward third base. The only play was at first. The stage was set. It was now runners on second and third with two outs. It was simple. The runners would be running on contact so any hit would win the game. Any out and the game was over. To make things interesting, the opponent's most powerful hitter was coming up. He was big and strong but slow running, so all bets were on something in the outfield.

After taking a couple of pitches the batter found one he liked. He gave a mighty rip and it was headed at Eric! Well, not exactly at him but over him! It was headed over his head and he knew it! This was a field with no home run fences. Nothing was automatic. Eric turned and began a full sprint as fast and hard as he could go. He looked back and saw the ball coming. He thought to himself, "I am not gonna make it!" But in a last desperate attempt, he stretched his gloved left hand above his head and right shoulder. To his amazement, he felt the ball hit his glove! He squeezed tightly on the snow cone catch. The thirteen-year-old kid was the hero of the men's league championship.

He often reflected on that moment as he grew older and he used it as an inspiration to go out and get involved against all odds in projects that sometimes seemed overwhelming. It was proof that miracles could happen due to diligence and hard work. You could beat the odds and make a difference.

The Practical
Joker in Me

I have long been known as a practical joker and for my off-beat sense of humor. I believe a smile is one of the best gifts I can give to anyone. I always try to make 'em laugh. It is the best part of me I have passed on to my kids as well, although it has started to come back to haunt me as I am now one of their favorite victims.

A recent success of my antics however, was at the expense of Eve. She is a very close friend who I confide in about a variety of subjects. We have long conversations about anything under the sun.

The nature of her job allows me to call her sometimes at work. Our talks are sometimes briefly interrupted by someone coming into her office, but her primary duties seem to involve paperwork. I have noticed that she sometimes is wearing a telephone headset so that she can continue to type or do other things while she talks. This was an opportunity too good to pass up.

On those occasions when I was on the phone with her and someone would come into her office to ask a question. I would be a good boy MOST of the time waiting patiently and not making a sound. But every once in a while I might make a brief comment in her ear just to try and catch her off guard trying to evoke a snicker. I was never quite successful but I was bound to get her to break.

Finally, one day a man she works with came in. I could hear him in the background. She was politely, professionally answering his query. I knew she was wearing the headset by the closeness of her voice. A perfect opportunity!

Right in the middle of her conversation with him, I planted the idea in her ear that she should ask him if he wanted to do the Hokey Pokey. She was a rock! What could I do to break this woman?! Then it hit me ... ."You put your right foot in. You put your right foot out. You put your right foot in and you shake it all about! ..."

That's right! I started singing the song in her ear. I was doing a vigorous wholehearted rendition of the Hokey Pokey on her headset while she was trying to keep her professional demeanor. After about five seconds I heard a SWISH ... SWISH ... SWOOK ... SWISH ... CRACK ... CRUMPH ... BAM! ... and all of the sudden her voice was distant.

She had hastily removed the headset. I could not control my laughter. While her conversation continued with this other person, I laughed till my face hurt and tears were running down my face. I had got her GOOD! Upon the end of her conversation with the man in her office, I heard the headset being replaced on her ear. This was immediately followed by "I am gonna kill you! You are so bad! I ripped out some hair getting that darned headset off." She then broke into uncontrollable laughter in reflection of her dilemma I had created.

She admitted that she had broken into a big smile and it was all she could do to keep from bursting into laughter with her co-worker in the room. She stated that never again would she trust me on the phone when someone was in the room. I counted this as a great victory and she has later admitted that it is a favorite moment of hers as well.

The 24 Hour Bug

The stomach bug is paying an unwelcome visit to my house this week. It has claimed three victims thus far and has left the other two of us with that "deer in the headlights" look, examining every little gurgle from our bellies watching for the first sign of impending doom.

This seems to be a twenty-four-hour type of bug. Well more like eighteen hours from first misery to reintroduction to some sort of foodstuffs more significant than a dry cracker. It is a place to which we all have been at various times in our lives and to which we never look forward to returning. Funny how we can so readily embrace that same toilet that is normally regarded as a bastion of germs the rest of our lives.

Of course being at home is the greatest blessing in the world when one of these episodes strikes. They are virtually impossible to plan for since they usually strike with a vengeance and with little or no warning. Most of us have a horror story or two about being somewhere less than inviting when the feeling hits you.

My most memorable stomach bug moment occurred one spring day at the construction site of a new home where I was working. I had arrived feeling perfectly normal at about 8:30am. I proceeded to run sound wiring through the rafters of the framed up structure. At about 10:00am I suddenly began to feel a nauseated feeling and abdominal cramps accompanied by a cold sweat, chills, a headache and weakness. I could feel what was coming and not a bathroom anywhere in sight. I struggled to load my tools and supplies into my car feeling worse by the minute. I knew my work day was done and I knew I needed to find a bathroom and fast!

About three miles down the road at the edge of town was a restaurant. I stumbled my way in just in time. Round one was now complete. I would have given all I had to be at home right then. Trouble was, home was 50 miles of suburban driving away. That was the longest 50 miles of my life. I stopped to contaminate half a dozen other businesses along the way and after what seemed like a week and a half, I finally made it home. Exhausted, but home to gladly spend my twenty-four hours having my affair with the toilet.

Sledding

Growing up in Pennsylvania, I have seen a good bit of snow. I have spent many days and nights sled riding, ice skating, and snowball fighting. It was a big part of being a kid there. It was also the source of some good memories.

There were two sleds of preference. One was a toboggan sled which would hold approximately six to eight people. These were great for long, large hills when lots of people were around. You could haul a crowd down a hill in a hurry. The other favorite was the rubber tire inner tube. Today's tubeless tires have made these a dying breed, but they were great fun, especially the ones from tractor tires. They were large enough to hold three or four people or you could lay back and ride solo. Inner tubes were great for hills with rough terrain or turns. They would absorb shock and maneuver fairly well.

Becky was a girl my age who lived probably half a mile up the road and she has the misfortune of being involved in two of my favorite sledding stories. She and I went to school together for twelve years and though we were never best friends or anything, we got along fine and often ended up playing together as part of a group of neighborhood kids. Behind her house was a large, long pasture field which came down to a wooden plank fence just behind her house. You could take a toboggan to the top and ride a good long ride. The only thing was that you had to physically stop before crashing into the fence. The hill would have continued another hundred yards down through their lawn if not for that darned fence.

One night several of us were riding down this hill in the dark making trip after trip in the fresh snow. It was one of those crisp, clear winter nights where the moon and stars provided enough light for you to see just a smidge. Each trip down was ended with the driver yelling "Fence!" and the rear rider dragging their feet to slow the sled while the others all jumped off. Anybody riding a toboggan knows that the driver can sometimes get a face full of snow when you slam into a drift or a snow bank. On one particular trip with Becky driving as the sled catapulted down the hill, the snow flew up blinding her. By the time she had cleared her eyes, the only thing she could say was "DUCK!" We were right upon the fence! There was no time to jump. We all hit the deck laying as low as possible bracing for the crash. A toboggan has a front that curls up in kind of a laid down U shape. Much to our amazement, all we heard was a little "Click" as the top of the front of the sled barely grazed the bottom plank of the fence. Even though our hearts were in our throats, we were ecstatic to find that we hade made it as we continued all the way to the bottom of the hill. From then on, we always rode right through the fence. I guess we were too young and foolish to worry about what might have happened if we had met a fencepost.

Poor Becky was at my house riding inner tubes one afternoon when her next mishap occurred. The hill at our house had little mounds and bumps and flattened out at the bottom near our garage. The space for the garage had been dug out of the hillside and you could choose to stop behind it, or if your aim was good, you could continue riding down to the driveway past the side of the garage. The snow was wet and the sledding path became more icy with each trip down the hill. Becky took her turn on the tractor tube and went flying. She was aiming for the swath that went to the driveway but she was carrying too much speed and try as she might, she did not quite make the turn. Instead she went sideways down the embankment that led to the garage wall and got wedged in there good and tight between the inner tube, the wall, and the bank. We expected her to come up out of there, but instead all we heard were her muffled cries for help. We asked her if she was hurt, she said "No, but get me out of here!" After laughing for a bit, we finally helped poor red-faced Becky from her predicament.

My best friend is responsible for some good snow memories too. In deep snow you have to make a sled trail a little at a time. You make several trips up and down the hill riding a little further each time. We were in the middle of this process when he went flying down the hill on his tube and flew right into a big snowdrift. He came up out of there looking like a snowman. The snow was freezing to his face. He took off running in a full sprint for home to get in front of the fire. All I could do was sit there and laugh.

He got his revenge. Not long afterwards, we were having a snowball fight. I had taken refuge in a drainage ditch which provided me great coverage while I made new ammunition. I had him pinned down with only a small bank for protection. I was pelting him at will with my icy concoctions, but with a plan and a stroke of luck, he got the last laugh. He began to time my appearances above the horizon. When he thought he had me figured out, he let one go as hard and fast as he could. I popped my head up just in time to meet my fate. It hit me square in the mouth and nose. I had blood pouring from everywhere. It was now my turn to run for the house.

One summer we got a toy called a summersled. It was a flat sled looking thing with wheels on the bottom. It really worked well. At least until my cousins came to visit. My brother, my three cousins and I took turns riding three at a time on that sled down the hill one summer night. To make it more interesting, the driver had to wear sunglasses in the dark! We must have made a hundred trips down that hill. We had a blast. But there was no fun to be had the next day when our father saw the big path down the middle of the yard where we had worn away all the grass. So came the end of our summer sledding days.

Sally

Sally came into my life about 18 months ago. She was a little bit late. I had spent 44 years looking for her. I did not really realize it was her I was seeking, but once I found her I knew. It was one of those moments they call an epiphany, a light bulb moment. The bond between us was instant and I firmly believe permanent. "We just knew" is the only way to describe it, no doubts, no maybes, no turning and running for your life.

We had a fairytale romance. We had meetings in lots of exotic places. We shared our hearts and souls and became in a way as one spiritually and emotionally. We were married last September in a beautiful ceremony and have spent many love filled days together as we look forward to sharing the next 50 years. This is all very true, but wait, let me back up. I seem to have skipped a few details. Sally and I spent the majority of our first date in a Meijer parking lot. In case you don't know, Meijer is a discount grocery and department store. We were late for our own wedding. The preacher looked like a mountain man. We now have seven children. And she has taught me that pooping on the floor is wrong.

Our new life is needless to say, interesting. Every time I turn around that woman is popping out another kid! No really, the actual truth about seven kids is that I was a single dad raising three kids alone and she was a single mom raising four … .til the one day when the lady met this fellow, and they knew that it was much more than a hunch … dee dum dum dum … .oops, sorry, anyhow, we knew it would be a challenge to join forces and become a family of nine plus two dogs and four cats, but we knew it was what we wanted so we jumped in, rolled up our sleeves and got busy putting together two families into one.

As for the wedding, we knew WHERE we wanted to be married. It was a beautiful state park where we had spent our 2nd date. We picked out a location and a date. The one problem we faced was that we did not know a minister in that area, so we went online and found a listing for a wedding chapel in the area. Sally made contact and arranged for the minister to come to the park to perform the ceremony. Everything was arranged. What could possibly go wrong?

Well besides flooding thunderstorms that is! The day of our wedding brought drenching, incessant downpours. This was cause to move the wedding indoors to the chapel where the preacher was from. Did I mention that we did not meet the preacher until five minutes after the ceremony was to begin? Well you try getting a bride and a groom and seven children ready for a wedding and then driving 50 miles in a downpour and being on time! The guests probably thought we had gained some last minute sanity!

Anyhow, here we are, running late, pulling into the parking lot of this "church" in the pouring rain. There was this poor guy out there directing cars where to park, totally drenched. What a crappy job! So, we all get out and run around to the back of the church through the muddy yard … .oh, by the way, the front entrance was closed because some old woman had accidentally driven her car through it the previous Sunday. But back to the story … We go inside, Sally and I finish getting ready, we are about to start the ceremony, the car parking guy comes up to me to introduce himself … ..Yep! He was the preacher, shoulder length hair, three teeth and all! The truth is that he turned out to be a very nice man and our wedding from that point went off without a hitch. A beautiful moment shared with this wonderful woman I love so dearly.

So there you have it! The basic story of how Sally came to be my Mrs. Oh, so you still want to know about pooping on the floor? Well, don't you think it is wrong too? Ok, ok, as Paul Harvey would say, "Here is the rest of the story."

Two of Sally's children have special needs. They have unique challenges that make their worlds quite different from ours. Elaine is Sally's 13-year-old daughter. She is deaf and legally blind with mild to moderate mental retardation. Elaine creates joy in anyone's life she touches, including mine. She is one very special young lady. Because of her disabilities, Elaine cannot enjoy many of the activities in which other children partake. She gets no benefit from music, or TV, or computers, or most toys. As it turns out, her greatest passion is her backyard swing. She swings several times each day. It almost appears to be a need for her as much as a want. It brings great joy to her life.

Another part of being Elaine is that she does not get the normal social cues that the rest of us do. She only learns what is presented directly to her. She does not learn much from the interactions of others. One struggle we have encountered with her from time to time is with going to the bathroom when she needs to rather than having an "accident" on herself. The big problem is when she has an "accident," she just takes her clothes off right there! No matter where "there" is!

As a way to try to change this behavior, Sally tried a new approach. She told Elaine, "If you poop on the floor, you cannot swing." This whole idea went over like a lead balloon! No swing!!! The horror of it all! Sure enough, one day soon after, Elaine had an accident. The swing was made "unavailable."

Elaine's primary language is American Sign Language (ASL). She would sign, "Swing!" Sally would sign, "Poop on the floor is wrong! Poop in potty and then you can swing!" Elaine would run to the potty and try with all her might to no avail. She would again sign "Swing!"

Mom would again sign, "Poop on the floor is wrong! Poop in the potty and then you can swing!" This went on for days!!!! It must have seemed like months to Elaine! For me it became my most well learned sign language to date. I can sign poop on the floor is wrong faster than anything else I know in ASL.

In the end Elaine pooped in the potty. She got to go back to swinging. Sally cried happy tears. And all was right with the world. And all continues to be right in our world. It may not be a typical world, but it is our world and we love it. I see my new family as a great blessing. A wonderful gift in the middle of this beautiful life between the raindrops.